Audrey
in Paris

Published in 2024 by Welbeck

An imprint of Welbeck Non-Fiction Limited,
part of Welbeck Publishing Group.

Offices in: London – 20 Mortimer Street, London W1T 3JW &
Sydney – Level 17, 207 Kent St, Sydney NSW 2000 Australia

www.welbeckpublishing.com

ISBN 978 1 80279 609 4

Editor: Isabel Wilkinson/ Heather Boisseau
Design: Russell Knowles
Picture research: Paul Langan
Production: Marion Storz

Printed in China

10 9 8 7 6 5 4 3 2 1

Audrey in Paris

THE FASHION ICON IN THE CITY OF LIGHT

Caroline Young

WELBECK

Contents

Audrey's Favourite Places

Explore the Paris of Audrey Hepburn, from walks along the banks of the River Seine and up the steep cobbled streets of Montmartre, to shopping in the eighth arrondisement and lunch at La Grande Cascade in the Bois de Boulogne.

38 Rue Parmentier

Hôtel Raphaël

Théâtre Vrai Guignolet

Lasserre Restaurant

VRAI GVIGNOLET

GIVENCHY

ANGELINA

Givenchy Salon

Angelina Café

Maxim's Restaurant

La Grande Cascade Restaurant

Givenchy's House

Wine Merlot

The Ritz
Paris

Place de
L'Opéra

Comédie Française
theatre

Jardin du
Palais-Royal

Arc de
Triomphe
du Carrousel

The Louvre

L'Orangerie
Restaurant

Pont au Double

17 Rue Malebranche

Orly Airport

AÉROPORT DE PARIS   ORLY

Introduction

"PARIS ISN'T FOR CHANGING PLANES.
IT'S FOR CHANGING YOUR OUTLOOK!
FOR THROWING OPEN THE WINDOWS
AND LETTING IN ... LETTING IN
LA VIE EN ROSE."

AUDREY HEPBURN IN *SABRINA*

PREVIOUS Audrey gazing over the city
from the highest point of Montmartre,
during the making of *Funny Face* in 1956.

In *Funny Face*, Audrey models in front of the
luxury La Flèche d'Or (The Golden Arrow)
train at the Gare du Nord.

FROM THE TIME SHE WALKED INTO THE
ATELIER OF THE YOUNG DESIGNER HUBERT
DE GIVENCHY, AND WITH HER TAKING ROLES
IN A NUMBER OF STARRY PARIS-SET MOVIES,
AUDREY HEPBURN EMBRACED THE BEAUTY
AND ELEGANCE OF THE CITY.

A udrey, and her movies, including *Sabrina* (1954), *Funny Face*
(1957) and *Charade* (1963), depict a sense of magic and
enchantment, that anything is possible in this most romantic
of cities. Her place as a timeless style icon is defined through
moments in Paris as captured on celluloid; dancing in a smoky
Left Bank club, running down the steps of the Louvre in a brilliant
red gown, dancing with Fred Astaire at the Eiffel Tower and
driving to The Ritz Paris in a sports car.

As Paris recovered from the trauma of occupation during the
Second World War, there was a new sense of excitement and renewal
in the air, particularly after Christian Dior showed his extravagant
"New Look" collection in 1947, which embraced femininity after wartime austerity. Paris was, by the mid-1950s, once again the world
leader in fashion. Coco Chanel had made a dramatic comeback in
1954 with her famous tweed suits and little black dress, Cristóbal
Balenciaga was leading in technical innovation with his radical
silhouettes and a new designer, Hubert de Givenchy, was making a
name for himself with cutting-edge simplicity.

Post-war Hollywood had a European outlook as more films were
shot on location to portray the romance of the Continent and
reflected the new democratization of travel. Hollywood's film studios
in the early fifties looked to Europe to find young, sophisticated stars

and Audrey Hepburn, a Belgian-born dancer, was hailed as a fresh talent with her film debut, *Roman Holiday* (1953). Her discovery was credited to celebrated French author Colette, who saw her as the embodiment of her young Parisian heroine Gigi, with her elfin features and innate sense of style.

After filming *Roman Holiday* in Rome, Audrey starred in *Sabrina* (1954), which was a Cinderella story for the 1950s – fulfilling the fantasy of going to Paris for the summer and returning as a captivating sophisticate. Audrey, a relative unknown, arrived at Givenchy's Paris salon dressed in Capri pants, a white T-shirt and ballet slippers, and from there she became the designer's muse – representing the sophistication and frivolity of Paris at the time. She returned to the city for *Funny Face* (1957) and *Love in the Afternoon* (1957) as her bright eyes and warm smile captured the excitement of being in love in the City of Light. She was one of the biggest stars in the world, yet she seemed as if she would be perfectly at home nibbling on a croissant or sipping a *café au lait* in one of the many Parisian cafés.

For Audrey, it was Givenchy who she felt fully understood her and made her feel at ease in her body, and women who wished to copy the Hepburn look rushed to the designer's breathtakingly elegant salon on Avenue George V. The simplicity of Audrey's natural style was quite revolutionary for an era when women were expected to be voluptuously compliant.

After *Breakfast at Tiffany's* (1961), Audrey would enter into a jazzier period which reflected the modernism of the 1960s, and would be played out in Paris, where there was a youthful sense of expression in the air. Stanley Donen's *Charade* (1963), a stylish thriller starring Cary Grant, marked her transition into sixties modishness in Givenchy hats and funnel-neck wool coats, as they adventure in a winter cityscape.

Audrey being fitted for couture by Hubert
de Givenchy at his salon in 1958.

In *How to Steal a Million* (1966), she zips around Paris with Peter O'Toole in a sports car, her up-to-the-minute wardrobe contrasting with the sober history of the Cathédrale Notre-Dame. In *Paris When It Sizzles* (1964), she is a secretary who helps William Holden write a Hollywood screenplay in two days. Their imagination wanders in Paris, as the city becomes their playground, with the Eiffel Tower and the Bois de Boulogne the backdrop to their colourful fantasies and growing romance.

By the late sixties Audrey reflected the countercultural fashions and embraced the French New Wave with *Two for the Road* (1967). Ironically, her own marriage to fellow actor Mel Ferrer was disintegrating at the same time and she punctuated this new chapter in her life with a daringly short and angular haircut by Alexandre de Paris, while wearing a new wardrobe of hip French designers

"AUDREY'S TIMELESS APPEAL IS FOREVER LINKED WITH PARIS"

like Michèle Rosier and Paco Rabanne. Later, as she focused on her humanitarian work for UNICEF, she would still return to Paris to visit her favourite places – Maxim's restaurant, and of course, Givenchy's salon.

As reality and film fantasy blended into one, Audrey's enduring appeal is forever linked with Paris. She was beloved by audiences for her natural elegance, the kindness that radiated from her, and for her easy sense of style that was so perfectly at home in the fashion capital. So, follow in the footsteps of Audrey, explore the city through her eyes and find that little bit of Paris magic for yourself.

In *How to Steal a Million* (1966), Audrey was
a Paris Mod icon, zipping around the city in
an open-top sports car.

CHAPTER ONE

Dreaming of Paris

AUDREY HEPBURN NEVER LIVED IN PARIS,
YET IT WAS AS IF SHE WAS MADE FOR THE
CITY. HER GAMINE FEATURES AND HER
NATURAL SENSE OF STYLE JUST SEEMED
TO CONVEY PARISIAN CHIC.

She expressed a preference for simplicity in how she dressed: a white shirt tied at the waist, a pair of cropped cigarette trousers or Capri pants and ballet slippers, or a clean-lined cocktail dress in muted colours. Her clothes didn't overpower her, rather she wore them in the way that Coco Chanel dictated: that a woman should wear a dress, and not let the dress wear her. Audrey's accent placed her outside both America and the English class system – she might have been British, and indeed she was a citizen of that country, but there was something more continental about her. A certain *je ne sais quoi.*

Audrey burst into public consciousness in the early fifties, at a time when Paris was experiencing a transformation through regeneration. From 1940–44, it had been an occupied city, where untold horrors occurred, particularly on its Jewish population, and where its citizens suffered food shortages and fear of reprisal under the Nazis. When the Allies swept into Paris in August 1944 to liberate the city from the brutal regime, they were given a rapturous reception by its defiant citizens, many of whom had supported the underground Résistance. During this time American culture converged with French, as GI soldiers stationed in the freed city brought to Paris the symbols of their culture: Coca-Cola, Lucky Strike cigarettes and swing music, while they took snaps of themselves by the Eiffel Tower and Notre-Dame and queued to buy bottles of Chanel No.5 for their sweethearts back home.

In June 1947, the United States announced a new provision for overseas aid called the European Recovery Programme, which became known as the Marshall Plan after the Secretary of State, George C. Marshall. It provided financial support to the European countries that had been broken by war, in particular the Axis powers of Italy, West Germany and Austria, as a means of unifying the continent and making these countries feel like they were no longer enemies. Britain and France also received funding to help them rise from the blitzed-out wreckage. In this period of renewal, as Paris

PREVIOUS The epitome of Parisian
elegance, Audrey views Paris from a bateau
mouche on the Seine in 1962.

Audrey conveyed classic Parisian gamine
chic with her short hair and black sweaters,
pictured here in 1955.

regained its place as the fashion capital of the world, the pretty streets and historic buildings were once again a lure for overseas visitors.

Paris benefited from a post-war wave of tourists who wished to experience the city's famous sights, which had somehow miraculously survived the war. It had been close; when the Germans were pushed out of Paris in August 1944 as the Allies advanced, dictator Adolf Hitler had given orders for the city to be destroyed and explosives were placed at its bridges and landmarks. His military governor in Paris, Dietrich von Choltitz, disobeyed orders because he believed it was futile to destroy such culture and on 25 August, von Choltitz surrendered the German garrison to the Free French government. As writer Gertrude Stein proclaimed in an issue of *Harper's Bazaar*, Paris is "all lovely and saved".

Paris has long held a fascination for Americans and in the years after the First World War, a group of artists and hedonists known as the Lost Generation flocked to the city to try to blot out their wartime experiences. This café society lived cheaply and decadently, in a city that was placed as the cultural centre of the world. It was the era of F. Scott and Zelda Fitzgerald, Ernest Hemingway and Pablo Picasso, and they gathered in the cafés, salons and absinthe bars of Montmartre and Montparnasse. "If you are lucky enough to have lived in Paris as a young man then wherever you go for the rest of your life, it stays with you, for Paris is a moveable feast," Hemingway wrote in his memoir.

In the late forties, Paris once again attracted young idealists, where the existentialist movement led by Jean-Paul Sartre and Simone de Beauvoir offered a philosophical insight into the human condition, where freedom could be found in individuality. *LIFE* magazine in 1952 carried a feature on the phenomenon of teenage Americans in Paris, with images by ground-breaking African-American photographer

PREVIOUS: GIs waiting outside Coco Chanel's rue Cambon salon to get hold of bottles of Chanel No.5 perfume.

A pretty cobbled Montmartre street in the early 1950s.

Gordon Parks. He depicted this tribe of young people experiencing the city as a playground. They drank Coca-Cola in jazz clubs, sat at sidewalk cafés on the Champs-Élysées, took the streetcar past the Arc de Triomphe and made exclamations such as "Quel Babes!" a decade before Audrey's Holly Golightly would utter similar pronouncements in *Breakfast at Tiffany's*. The article declared:

"NEITHER BOYS NOR GIRLS THINK MUCH OF FROGS' LEGS, BUT THEY KNOW EVERY PLACE IN PARIS THAT MAKES HAMBURGERS AND HOT DOGS AND, WHILE HAVING A SNACK AT A SIDEWALK CAFÉ, ARE INCLINED TO DREAM OF THE CORNER DRUGSTORE."

Visitors to the city held a romantic, postcard vision of Paris forged from watching Hollywood movies, with accordion players in berets on street corners, and where the Eiffel Tower was the ultimate symbol of Paris. Gustave Eiffel's creation shimmers at night, guiding visitors around the city with its twinkling lights, while reinforcing the idea of Paris as the City of Love.

The Eiffel Tower was marketed from the moment it was unveiled at the 1889 Exposition Universelle and made its first screen appearance in the 1924 René Clair silent film *Paris Qui Dort* (*Paris Asleep*). From then on, an American film set in Paris wasn't complete without a glimpse of the Eiffel Tower. Not only is Paris one of the most cinematic cities, but it is also the birthplace of the motion picture, when on 28 December 1895, the first public screening of a film took place at the Grand Café on Boulevard des Capucines.

There had been a long-held belief in Hollywood that any place in the world could be recreated on a studio backlot with a skilled team of set designers and scenarists. Hollywood productions that featured the city typically created an idealized image through an American viewpoint. This included Ernst Lubitsch's *Ninotchka* (1939), *An American in Paris* (1951), *Gentlemen Prefer Blondes* (1953), *Gigi* (1958) and Audrey's first Paris-set film, *Sabrina* (1954).

The perfect backdrop for fashion shoots in the 1950s, as depicted in the film *Under the Paris Sky* (or *Sous Le Ciel de Paris*) in 1951.

Leslie Caron and Gene Kelly in *An American
in Paris* (1951), which inspired a new
generation of visitors to Paris.

The wartime experience had expanded the horizons of the hundreds of thousands of young people posted overseas and with newspapers and newsreels bringing images of Europe directly into people's homes, American audiences were becoming worldlier in their outlook. They hoped for realism when it came to seeing foreign locales on screen.

In the years after the Second World War, the American film industry increasingly upped sticks and came to Europe to shoot movies on location. This was for a number of financial and aesthetic reasons. The movie studios were attracted by the cheaper production costs of using local crews and the tax breaks that came with it, as well as being able to access the profits that had been frozen by European governments during the war. They also wished to capture the exoticism of being in an actual city, rather than on a set with painted backdrops.

By 1950 Rome had become known as "Hollywood on the Tiber" due to the sheer number of American productions being made in the city. Hollywood filmmakers were inspired by the Italian neorealists like Roberto Rossellini and Vittorio de Sica who, out of wartime necessity, used real locations and filmed on a tight budget to create gritty works including *Rome, Open City* (1945) and *Bicycle Thieves* (1948). Audrey Hepburn's *Roman Holiday*, made over the summer of 1952, was one of the first American productions to wholly take advantage of location shooting by filming entirely in Rome. It was followed by *Three Coins in the Fountain* in 1954, a romance about three American women enjoying the sun-soaked piazas of Rome. While Vincent Minnelli's *An American in Paris* (1951) was filmed exclusively on MGM's lot in Los Angeles, despite lead star Gene Kelly trying to persuade the studio otherwise, its huge success placed Paris in the minds of audiences and filmmakers.

By the early fifties, Hollywood was struggling to compete with the growing popularity of television and the studios invested in new film technologies with the aim of retaining their audiences. Processes like Technicolor, VistaVision and Cinemascope really allowed for the romantic cityscapes of Rome and Paris to pop on screen. It was in these conditions that Audrey Hepburn came to be captured on celluloid among Paris's most brilliant landmarks. In the fifties she starred in sweet escapism – *Sabrina, Love in the Afternoon,* and *Funny Face.* By 1960, New Wave filmmakers like François Truffaut, Jean-Luc Godard and Louis Malle were shaking up the industry and changing the way characters used the city. This group of former film critics admired the mise-en-scène of classic Hollywood cinema, but aimed to shift filmmaking from the studio to the street, using real apartments, Métro cars and cafés, and where they depicted young people roaming free in Paris. In Louis Malle's *Zazie dans le Métro* (1960), for example, a young girl makes a journey across Paris to visit the Eiffel Tower. In Jean-Luc Godard's *À Bout de Souffle* (Breathless, 1960), Jean Seberg

"I NEVER WANT TO GO HOME. I LOVE PARIS!"

AUDREY HEPBURN IN *FUNNY FACE*

wanders the boulevards of Paris selling issues of the *New York Herald Tribune*, with her criminal boyfriend, played by Jean-Paul Belmondo.

As Paris was a backdrop for their stylistic experimentalism, American filmmakers once again followed suit with a further preference for real locations. In this period Audrey was frequently in the city to make *Paris When It Sizzles, Charade* and *How to Steal a Million,* and in France for *Two for the Road.*

Young college-age women, with an eye for adventure, spent summers travelling in Europe, and by the mid-fifties, the hope of seeing Audrey in a bistro or strolling along the banks of the Seine was part of Paris's appeal. The city at that time existed in a fantasy realm. It was a place of high fashion and majestic landmarks, of pavement cafés where one could read the works of Émile Zola or Jean-Paul Sartre over a steaming *café au lait,* a *citron pressé* or a glass of Pernod, with its herbal scent, and pop into patisseries for fresh, buttery croissants or delicate *mille-feuilles.* There was Montmartre, with its sloping cobbled streets and gas-lit steps leading up to the white domed Sacre-Coeur, and with the street artists a reminder of its history as the quarters of artists like Henri de Toulouse-Lautrec and Vincent van Gogh. There was the eternal presence of the Eiffel Tower sparkling by the river Seine at night, or the Gothic Notre-Dame cathedral with its gargoyles, where one could image the "Hunchback" in its bell tower, as depicted by Charles Laughton in the 1939 film, and Anthony Quinn in the 1956 version.

"I remember the fifties as a time of renewal and of regained security," Audrey would later say. "There was a rebirth of opportunity, vitality and enthusiasm – a return to laughter and gaiety – the world was functioning again. Above all, there was a wonderful quality of hope, born from relief and gratitude for those greatest of all luxuries – freedom and peace." [1]

San Franciscan author Beverley Lehman West spent a year in Paris after college in the early fifties, to fulfil a deep desire to experience this "magical city where they danced in the streets, whiled away hours in cafés, and scribbled masterpieces on the Left Bank". As she wrote in her memoirs, *Finding My Way Back to 1950s Paris*: "Even poverty seemed to be romantic in Paris."[2]

The post-war city was advertised as a fabled place of glamour and romance, but its outward image covered up the cracks in its foundations and the peeling paint on its walls. In 1951, the same year that Gene Kelly and Leslie Caron danced together in *An American in Paris*, France's trade unions were organizing general strikes for all types of workers across the city. A young American, Ann Montgomery, arrived in Paris in 1954 to work as a high fashion model, and in her account of her time, *Another Me: A Memoir* (2008), she described how Paris was still suffering from "a war-weary shabbiness that cast a despairing shadow over the grandeur of the ancient city." [3]

29

In half of Audrey's Paris-set films, she convincingly played a Parisienne, as she possessed the qualities that had long been assigned to its women. In 1910, writer Octave Uzanne described the Parisian woman as "an aristocrat among the world's women", and in popular culture, from paintings and advertising to literature and movies, her image was reinforced as the personification of beauty, elegance and allure. She came in a number of guises. There was the fashion plate in couture by Charles Worth and Paul Poiret, the seductive coquette and the gamine with her boyish haircut, her mischievous charm and her androgynous style.

After the war, the Parisian woman was praised for her in-vogue thinness, but her emaciated frame had been borne of the acute food shortages during the conflict. When Christian Dior unveiled his extravagant New Look collection, there was still rationing in place for bread and other food staples, as well as for coal and electricity.

Audrey personified these notions of the Parisian woman in her movies, particularly with her cropped hair and slim body, which in turn reflected her own wartime horrors of malnutrition. Still, her films offered a respite from reality and that's what she adored about them too. She liked the fantasy world of her movies and the magic that only Paris could weave. It was the place where Audrey Hepburn, the elegant gamine, was created.

During one of her early visits to Paris in 1952, as a fledgling actress on the cusp of fame, she discovered a young designer, Hubert de Givenchy, who had only recently established his own label. When he was asked to create Hepburn's costumes for her second Hollywood film, *Sabrina*, it would be the beginning of a designer and muse relationship that helped establish Audrey as a fashion icon. And it was a Parisian writer, Colette, and her story about a young cocotte, *Gigi*, that first introduced the actress to the world.

Audrey and then-husband Mel Ferrer
observe a fashion show at Givenchy's first
atelier, close to Parc Monceau.

CHAPTER TWO

The Gamine of Paris

AUDREY PERFECTLY REPRESENTED ALL THAT
WAS PARISIAN, YET SHE WAS, IN FACT, BORN
IN BRUSSELS, TO A DUTCH BARONESS – ELLA
VAN HEEMSTRA – AND A BRITISH-IRISH BANKER
FATHER, JOSEPH HEPBURN-RUSTON. AUDREY
KATHLEEN HEPBURN-RUSTON CAME INTO THE
WORLD ON MAY 4, 1929 AND BECAUSE BOTH
HER PARENTS WERE BRITISH CITIZENS, SHE
BECAME ONE TOO.

Her early years were spent in Belgium, Holland (the Netherlands) and then England, where she was sent at the age of five. "I lived and was based in Belgium until I moved to Holland, so my first words were French, but I spent a lot of time in England," she told *Vanity Fair* in 1991. "My mother couldn't afford an English nanny, and she wanted me to speak English, so she would send me every summer to stay with a family I absolutely adored." [4]

She was just six years old when her father walked out on the family a few years before the Second World War broke out in Europe in September 1939, leaving behind a devastated wife and daughter. Audrey would credit it as one of the most traumatic experiences of her life, and said that the event tortured her "beyond measure". [5]

When war was declared, Audrey's mother Ella mistakenly believed that it would be safer to return to her home in Arnhem than to stay in Britain, which was expected to be ravaged by bombs and faced the possibility of invasion. However, Germany ignored the neutrality of Holland and in May 1940, its forces swept into the country and occupied it for the next four years. During this time, the Dutch people experienced unimaginable horrors. By 1944 over 100,000 Dutch Jews had been sent to German concentration camps and ultimately a third of the Jewish population was murdered by the regime. Audrey's half-brother Ian Quarles van Ufford, a member of the Dutch Resistance, was arrested by the Germans and for the entirety of the war, the family were unaware that he was still alive.

Ever since she attended her first ballet in Brussels, Audrey had dreamed of being a ballerina. Despite the disruption of war, she took classes at Arnhem Conservatory of Music and Dance and the wonder of dance offered her moments of escape. These skills also proved to be a useful cover for helping the Dutch Resistance. She put on performances in private homes to raise money for the underground movement and as she walked to and from the conservatory for her ballet lessons, she hid notes in her wooden shoes to pass on to members of the Dutch Resistance to help in their sabotage of the occupying forces.

In the 1952 film *Secret People*, Audrey was able to display her skills in ballet.

PREVIOUS Audrey. photographed by Sam Shaw in a bustling Paris café in 1957.

Despite the hope instilled by the Allies storming the beaches of Normandy and slowly pushing their way through Europe, the harsh winter of 1944 was particularly grim. Serious food shortages meant there was little else to eat but turnips and tulip bulbs, and by the end of the war, 16-year-old Audrey was suffering the symptoms of malnutrition: "I came out of the war thankful to be alive, aware that human relationships are the most important thing of all, far more than wealth, food, luxury, careers, or anything you can mention," she later said. [6]

The horrors of war stayed with her for the rest of her life, having witnessed the brutal treatment dished out by the Nazis and the relentless round-ups on the streets of men, women and children to be taken to work camps, where they likely died by disease or in the gas chambers. She was haunted by the fate of her contemporary, diarist Anne Frank, who was hiding with her family in an attic in Amsterdam at the same time. Audrey felt deeply that she herself was lucky to have survived. Later, as she experienced the luxuries of being a movie star, of eating at the best restaurants in Paris and staying in beautiful hotels, she only needed to think back to the war to be grateful: "When you have had the strength to survive starvation, you never again send back a steak simply because it's under-done," she said. [7]

The family's considerable wealth had been lost in the war and so her mother worked as a cook and housekeeper to endure those first years of peacetime. Any money left over was put towards Audrey's dance lessons as the conflict hadn't killed her ambition to become a ballerina. As a child, Audrey often felt like an awkward duckling, but blossoming into adulthood, she was tall and very slender, with big eyes and a wide smile that lit up her face. At the age of 18 she made her film debut when cast in a small part as a KLM air stewardess in the movie *Dutch in Seven Lessons* (1948).

Audrey's devotion to dancing was rewarded when she received the good news that she had won a scholarship for the Rambert School of

In 1950 Audrey starred on the London stage in the comedy revue, *Sauce Piquante.*

Ballet and Contemporary Dance in London. Believing in this young girl's potential, Madame Rambert invited Audrey to stay with her at her London home. Despite her dedication, at 5ft 7 she was beginning to realize she was too tall to make it as a prima ballerina and she had also lost too much training time as a result of the war. Eager to earn a living, her free time was spent going to auditions for West End musicals, calling in on agents and working as a part-time model. The hard work paid off when she was one of a handful of girls selected from 3,000 hopefuls to join the chorus line of the musical *High Button Shoes* at London's Hippodrome in 1948. By the time the run ended in spring 1949, she knew her future wasn't in ballet, but she could use her performance skills in other ways. She possessed a unique star quality that helped her stand out among the other chorus girls.

The show's featured male dancer, Nickolas Dana, was struck by her natural flair for style, which she had honed through her modelling work. He'd noticed the clever ways she would play with the few items she had in her wardrobe – just one skirt, one blouse, one pair of shoes, and a beret, but with many different scarves. "She'd wear the little beret on the back of her head, on one side, on the other side – or fold it in two and make it look very strange. She had the gift, the flair of how to dress." [8]

It was during a performance of *High Button Shoes* that she was spotted by Cecil Landeau, a London producer looking to cast an international crowd for his new revue, *Sauce Tartare*. It opened in May 1949, at the Cambridge Theatre, and Audrey acted out a number of skits, including dressing up as a French maid in scenes set in the Pigalle district of Paris.

"I worked like an idiot," she said in 1991. "It was work, work, work, work. I did two shows at the same time, a musical revue at the Cambridge Theatre, twelve performances a week, and then we were all shipped to Ciro's nightclub right after the show, and there we did a floor show. And I was doing television. I did anything to earn a buck so that my mother could come over and join me."

Landeau cast Audrey in his follow-up show, *Sauce Piquante*, opening in April 1950, and her sophisticated continental appeal and those

Christian Dior's New Look was a fashion
revolution when launched in 1947.

PREVIOUS Audrey was excited to travel to the
Côte d'Azur to film *Monte Carlo Baby* in 1951.

beautiful eyes wowed the crowds and impressed a casting director from Ealing Studios. The meeting led to bit parts in a number of British films, including the 1951 film *Laughter in Paradise*, as a flirty cigarette girl, and in *The Lavender Hill Mob* (also 1951) with Alec Guinness. These small roles made such an impression that she won a seven-year contract with the Associated British Picture Corporation.

Next came her biggest role yet, in the film *Secret People* (1952), where she played a ballerina living as a refugee in London, and where she skilfully performed her own ballet dancing, *en pointe*, or on the tips of her toes. From here, she received an offer to play a spoilt actress in a comedy set on the Riviera, entitled *Monte Carlo Baby* (1951). It was to be made in English and French, and so Hepburn's fluency in both was one of the reasons for her casting. For Audrey, this lightweight film had many things going for it. For one, the languorous Côte d'Azur location, which she had always longed to visit, and secondly, she would get to wear a real Christian Dior dress on screen, which she would be allowed to keep.

Now that she was going to be in France for a number of weeks, she felt she needed to update her look and so she asked for her hair to be cropped into a pixie cut, giving her the appearance of a quirky, cool Parisian girl. At the end of May 1951, she and her mother travelled to the Riviera. On the way they stopped in Paris so she could be fitted for her costume at the House of Dior on 30 Avenue Montaigne, in the heart of the fashion district.

Christian Dior's phenomenal success following the launch of his first collection in 1947 perfectly represented Paris's recovery from the Second World War. "I wanted a house in which every single thing would be new," he said. "All around us, life was beginning anew: it was time for a new trend in fashion." He believed that "French couture would have to return to the traditions of great luxury." [9]

During the occupation many of Paris's prestigious designers had closed down their businesses and with acute shortages of fabric and manpower, and the halt of exports, the once lucrative fashion

Audrey enjoying the Riviera sunshine
during the filming of *Monte Carlo Baby.*

Audrey with the writer Colette in
1951, during the Broadway stage
production of *Gigi*.

industry struggled to continue. The wheels had been set in motion for its recovery in 1944, shortly after the liberation of Paris. Lucien Lelong, chairman of the Chambre Syndicale de la Couture, agreed to a fundraising exhibition where some of the top couturiers would create miniature outfits for dolls as textile rationing was still in force. The exhibition, entitled Théâtre de la Mode, used a theatre background, with sets designed by Jean Cocteau and Christian Bérard, and when it opened at the Louvre in March 1945, it enchanted the 100,000 visitors who came to see it and raised a million francs for war relief. The exhibition toured other cities in Europe before transferring to New York and San Francisco and the message was clear: France was still a fashion leader and it was welcoming to visitors.

When he launched his debut Spring/Summer 1947 collection, Christian Dior would prove to be the delight that marked the end of the war. During the occupation, women in Paris, living under heavy

"ALL AROUND US, LIFE WAS BEGINNING ANEW: IT WAS TIME FOR A NEW TREND IN FASHION."

CHRISTIAN DIOR

textile rationing, had taken to wearing boxy jackets, stacked shoes and huge hats and turbans. Dior's luxury collection was a return to the femininity of the past, with soft, round shoulders, padding on the bust and hips, nipped-in waists and yards of fabric. He named it "Corolle", after the open petals of the rose. Carmel Snow, editor of US *Harper's Bazaar*, proclaimed it "such a new look" and the name stuck. There was outrage in Paris at the amount of fabric required for his creations, given the continued scarcity of resources, and during a fashion shoot at the Lepic market in Montmartre, women stallholders, angered at the excess on display, attacked one of the Dior models, attempting to rip the clothes from her body. The models quickly sought safety in a nearby bar, and they, and their costumes, were driven back to Dior's salon on avenue Montaigne.

Despite these protests, Christian Dior was credited with making such an impact on French culture and economy that he was presented with the prestigious Légion d'Honneur in 1950. At the same time, Cristóbal Balenciaga was showing new silhouettes that had never been seen in women's fashion before. Almost overnight he earned a reputation as a master at cutting and manipulating fabric into abstract designs. One of his admirers was a young, and very tall, designer named Hubert de Givenchy, who considered the Spanish couturier to be "the complete creator". After learning his craft under the revolutionary Elsa Schiaparelli for four years, Givenchy opened his own salon in 1952, emerging onto the scene as Paris fashion was casting a spell once more and with Audrey Hepburn as an early champion.

But in the meantime, Audrey collected her dress from Dior and travelled to the Riviera to begin work on *Monte Carlo Baby*. She was filming a scene at the Hôtel de Paris in Monte Carlo one morning, at the same time as the writer Colette was being pushed through the lobby in her wheelchair, by her husband, Maurice Goudeket. The beautiful Hôtel de Paris, an ornate wedding cake of a building that represented the jollity of the Belle Époque era, was Colette's home away from home since 1908 and she was treated as the personal guest of Monaco's Prince Rainier himself.

Colette was famed for her series of risqué stories about the coquette schoolgirl Claudette, which were initially published under the pen name of her first husband, Henry Gauthier-Villars. A Paris libertine, he introduced her to the city's avant-garde circles at the turn of the century. Her time in Paris's salons with the bohemians, courtesans and intellectuals would shape her writing in the years to come, as her stories explored love and sexuality in the fin de siècle.

She wrote *Gigi* during the Nazi occupation of Paris as a means of escapism, by recreating the city at the turn of the century, when it had seemed to be full of beauty. The titular character is the gawky adolescent daughter of a soprano at the opera, who is expected to follow in the traditions of her family by becoming a courtesan and seducing a wealthy man. However, the sprightly Gigi wishes to follow her own heart rather than be confined as a mistress. In 1951 Anita Loos adapted it to a two-part stage play for Broadway and there was an international search to find an actress who possessed the same wide-eyed, coltish energy.

The elderly writer, distinctive with her cherry-red curls and bright lipstick, was being wheeled towards the dining room for breakfast when she was informed it was closed due to a production company using it for filming. Horrified at this interruption to her schedule, she ignored the edict and entered the room regardless. Here, she spotted Audrey as part of the film crew and was immediately struck by her presence. She had assumed she was 15 or 16 rather than her real age of 22 and said to her husband, "There is our Gigi for America."

After Colette made some enquiries, Audrey and her mother were introduced to the legendary writer and a private meeting was arranged for the next day. "My dear, I have just sent a cable to New York to tell

47

"THERE IS OUR GIGI FOR AMERICA"

WRITER COLETTE ON SPOTTING AUDREY FOR THE FIRST TIME

them to stop looking for a Gigi. I have found her," Colette told Audrey. She was absolutely thrilled at having been noticed by the famous writer, and was excited as to what might happen next.

The director of the play contacted Audrey in London so she could audition, and as soon as she was cast, her life was a whirl of interviews and there were further trips to Paris to be fitted for her stage costumes. After the show opened on Broadway in November 1951, it proved to be a critical and commercial success. *LIFE* magazine ran the headline, "Audrey Is a Hit", and by this time, she was already being sought by Paramount Pictures in Hollywood.

Director William Wyler was after a young actress to play a runaway princess in his new film, *Roman Holiday*. Elizabeth Taylor and Jean

Simmons had been considered, but neither was available, and rather than a star, he wanted a girl without an American accent, who possessed beauty and personality and who would be believable as a princess.

Richard Mealand, one of the producers at Paramount, had spotted Audrey's charming, but brief role in *Laughter in Paradise* (1951) and recommended her. "She is a little on the thin side, but very appealing," he wrote in a memo. "There is no question of her ability and she dances very well. Her speaking voice is clear and youthful with no extremes of accent. She looks more Continental than English." [10]

After impressing with her screen test, where she was so natural and at ease in front of the cameras, William Wyler was won over: "Everyone at the studio was very enthused about the girl and I am delighted we have signed her," he said. [11] With *Roman Holiday*, Audrey found herself in the unique situation of going from being a chorus girl to starring in smash-hit Broadway show *Gigi*, to winning the lead role in a major film.

The last performance of *Gigi* was on May 31, 1952 and the next day she flew to Paris with her fiancé, James Hanson, the son of a millionaire Huddersfield businessman, for a much-needed holiday en route to Rome. Audrey arrived in Italy 10 days later on a Pan Am flight from Paris, carrying her costumes for the movie with her to save Paramount import duty. The film captured the holiday spirit of those years after the war, where young people wanted to go out and see the world and to find excitement in simple pleasures. Audrey's Princess Ann, now hiding in Rome, wants to do "just whatever I like the whole day long ... to sit at a sidewalk café and look in shop windows, walk in the rain, have fun, and maybe some excitement."

On its release in August 1953, *Roman Holiday* and its novice star immediately captured the attention of the public. "This is the most delectable romantic comedy I have seen in years. What makes it so outstanding?" wrote Lionel Collier in *Picturegoer* magazine. "There's the

When *Gigi* opened at the Fulton Theatre on Broadway in 1951, Audrey was heralded as a promising talent.

graciousness and range of expression of Audrey Hepburn, who plays the heroine's part with a sweep that sends her soaring."

It was a fairy tale that matched the type of film Audrey would make a career out of – the transformational Cinderella stories of *Sabrina*, *Funny Face* and *My Fair Lady*. But she also reflected the same dreams and ambitions of all those adventurous young women in Paris and Rome, who were seeking a little more independence than the generations that came before.

One of the keys to the film's success was Hepburn's unique but accessible image. Hollywood glamour often seemed unattainable, but Audrey, with her cropped hair and her costume, designed by Paramount's Academy Award-winning Edith Head, was effortless and easy to replicate, with the long skirt cinched at the waist, the shirt with rolled-up sleeves and the jazzy necktie. This relaxed style helped to make her the new star for a new era. The moment in *Roman Holiday* that launched the Audrey Hepburn of legend was when Princess Ann visits a barber and asks him to chop off her long hair. Not since Greta Garbo's pageboy bob in the 1930s had a hairstyle captured the public's imagination and it came to represent the epitome of youth. Cecil Beaton observed in *Vogue* in 1954 that "Nobody ever looked like her before World War Two ... now thousands of imitations have appeared. The woods are full of emaciated young ladies with rat-nibbled hair and moon-pale faces." [12]

Audrey was placed as a direct opposite to her contemporary Marilyn Monroe, who was a rising star at the same time, and whose film *Gentlemen Prefer Blondes* would be released just a few months after *Roman Holiday*. Marilyn was voluptuous, blonde and ditzy, whereas Audrey was dark-haired, active and sophisticated. She was the girl next door, even if that girl had been raised in Paris.

Audrey with her co-star Gregory Peck at the Colosseum in Rome during the filming of *Roman Holiday* in 1952.

CHAPTER THREE

La Vie en Rose

FROM THE MOMENT *ROMAN HOLIDAY* WAS
RELEASED, AUDREY WOULD CONSTANTLY
BE REFERRED TO AS "GAMINE",
"DOE-EYED", AND "GAZELLE-LIKE" – WORDS
THAT REFLECTED HER INIMITABLE IMAGE.

The qualities she possessed were so different from the sex symbols and teen stars that were her contemporaries: "What they mean," she would later joke to husband Mel Ferrer, "is tall and skinny." [13]

Audrey had convincingly played a princess from an unnamed European country and it was as if she existed between continents; she wasn't French, but she seemed like she could be, and while she had a British passport, she didn't identify as such either. She also possessed a Hollywood charm, although she wasn't American. She was set apart from both the glamour of Rita Hayworth, Elizabeth Taylor, Lana Turner and Marilyn Monroe and the perky all-American girls like Debbie Reynolds and Natalie Wood. With her ballet training, she carried herself with a grace and dignity that went beyond her years.

"SABRINA WOULD ALSO FIND THAT A LITTLE BIT OF PARIS MAGIC COULD TRANSFORM HER LIFE"

55

Her talent had been so obvious in *Roman Holiday* that Paramount Pictures was eager to secure her follow-up and Audrey suggested an adaptation of Samuel Taylor's Broadway play, *Sabrina Fair*. The modern Cinderella story appealed to her as she felt a connection with this dreamy, but anxious girl, Sabrina Fairchild: "Sabrina was a dreamer who lived a fairytale and she was a romantic, an incorrigible romantic, which I am. I could never be cynical. I wouldn't dare. I'd roll over and die before that," said Audrey in 1980. "After all, I've been so fortunate in my own life – I feel I've been born under a lucky star." [14]

PREVIOUS In *Sabrina* (1954), a Givenchy suit transforms a mousy chauffeur's daughter into a stylish Parisian.

Photographed here by *Paris Match*, Audrey was at ease in the drawing rooms and salons of Paris.

Sabrina would also find that a little bit of Paris magic could transform her life. As the mousy daughter of the chauffeur for a grand Long Island family, she's consumed by the gnawing pain of unrequited love for their youngest son, David (William Holden). A playboy who has his seduction technique down to a fine art, he is completely oblivious to the young woman who stays above the garage. Thomas Fairchild (John Williams) has arranged for his daughter to go to Paris to train at the prestigious Cordon Bleu cooking school in the hope that it will help her to forget about her secret love: "It's not every girl who's lucky enough to go to Paris," he tells her. "And it's the best cooking school in the world."

Despite her reluctance to leave David, and following a half-hearted suicide attempt, Sabrina does as she's told and goes to Paris. At the Cordon Bleu cooking school, a very French chef in his white cap stands by a large, round window with a perfect view to the Eiffel Tower as he instructs his pupils on how to crack an egg. She is told by a fellow student, an older baron, that when people are happily in love, they burn their soufflés. And when people are unhappy, they forget to turn the oven on.

As she sits in her apartment in Paris, with the Sacré-Coeur Basilica and Montmartre visible outside her window, she thanks her father for what she describes as the two most wonderful years of her life. With her newly cropped hair and grown-up robe, she now appears effortlessly chic, having befriended the wealthy baron, who treats her like a daughter, takes her to the opera and the races, and introduces her to Parisian designers. She signs off her letter: "If you should have any difficulty recognizing your daughter, I shall be the most sophisticated woman at the Glen Cove station."

Waiting at the station for her father to collect her, Sabrina's new maturity is revealed through her tailored Parisian suit, white turban and simple hoop earrings. David just happens to be driving past and when he notices her beauty, he pulls up and offers to give her

Audrey's character Sabrina is taught how
to crack an egg at the famous Cordon Bleu
cookery school in Paris.

Writing a letter to her father, with a view of
La Basilique du Sacré Coeur, Montmartre,
from her window, a new, Parisian, Sabrina.

OVERLEAF Audrey with her co-star William
Holden during the making of *Sabrina*.

a lift in his car. The woman now dressed in a Givenchy suit, with a pile of suitcases and a French poodle, is so elegant that David, in fact, doesn't recognize her at first. He invites her to the extravagant summer ball that evening and she arrives as a vision of enchantment in a white strapless gown, its full skirts dipping around her, as she attracts admiring glances from David and the other male guests. His older brother Linus Larrabee (Humphrey Bogart), who is focused on another, more prosperous match for David, decides to seduce Sabrina himself, with the aim of sending her back to Paris. He knows how much the city means to her and how she found contentment there, particularly after she enthuses about its transformational qualities.

Linus plans to lure Sabrina onto a French ocean liner under the pretence he'll be joining her, then leave her with a generous compensation package so she can at least enjoy Paris by herself, and in style too. However, realizing his true feelings, he can't let her go alone and despite the age difference, the ending offers a sweet and satisfying conclusion as he joins her on the deck of the ship. Their union is chaste; there's no kiss at the end, instead they embrace. As co-script writer Ernest Lehman remembered, director Billy Wilder wanted to include a hint that Bogart had slept with Audrey, but Lehman was adamant in his refusal. "She was just a slip of a girl ... gentle and sweet ... He was furious at me for insisting they don't sleep with each other. I wouldn't give in on this point." [15]

It may have been a romantic comedy, but there's a melancholic undertone to the film and Audrey could relate to Sabrina's feelings of insecurity. "I lack self-confidence," she once said. "I don't know whether I shall ever get it. Perhaps it is better to be unsure of yourself, as I am. But it is very tiring." And just as Sabrina emerges from Paris a different woman, Audrey felt she had transformed herself with the right haircut and clothing, and by accentuating her eyes with kohl eyeliner and thick lashes. She also followed the discipline ingrained in her by her mother, who she recalled, "taught

me to stand straight, sit erect, use discipline with wine and sweets, and to smoke only six cigarettes a day."[16] Despite these early scenes set in Paris, the cast didn't set foot in France and instead the movie was filmed on Long Island and on the Paramount lot. It was agreed, however, that for her make-over, Audrey needed an elegant wardrobe from a real Parisian designer. As an unknown in her debut film *Roman Holiday*, Paramount's head costume designer Edith Head had full control over what Audrey would wear. She had been excited by the prospect of dressing the actress, who she described as a "leading lady looking like a Paris mannequin",[17] however she was bitterly disappointed when director Billy Wilder informed her that Audrey would be wearing a wardrobe purchased in France. In order to demonstrate the transformation of Sabrina, from naïve girl to woman, she needed to be a true Parisian sophisticate, wearing real French couture as an unspoken symbol of the blossoming awareness of her own sexual powers. Paris was often used as code for eroticism; the rosy memories of the Belle Époque era were of cabaret, can-can dancers and courtesans, and its people were considered to possess a more developed sensuality.

After completing *Roman Holiday*, Audrey had taken advantage of a gap in her schedule by booking a much-needed holiday in France with her mother. They visited Bordeaux and Biarritz, and with a stopover in Paris on the way, producers at Paramount decided this would be the perfect opportunity for her to pick up pieces for her on-screen wardrobe. Originally, they had suggested she visit the salon of Cristóbal Balenciaga as the designer wife of Paramount's executive in France, Gladys de Segonzac, hailed him as the pinnacle of Parisian style. One production memo noted that Mrs de Segonzac, "being in the Paris couture business, knows Paris clothes better than Miss Hepburn". [18]

Balenciaga had created a stir in 1950 as the antithesis of Christian Dior's New Look, where his designs were more linear and less

upholstered, and included such innovations as the balloon jacket and
the sack dress, which eradicated the traditional feminine silhouette.
Almost overnight he became internationally famous for his fluidity of
fabric and cut, and just as Dior's hourglass silhouette was a welcome
artifice in the post-war recovery, Balenciaga spoke to the modern,
active woman. He was, alongside Dior, the designer that an American
in Paris would likely covet.

When approached by producers at Paramount, Balenciaga insisted
he didn't have the capacity to meet the needs of the film – he was
too rushed to prepare the autumn collections. Audrey suggested
an alternative designer. With her pay cheque from *Roman Holiday*
she had purchased an off-the-rack coat by a young designer named
Hubert de Givenchy and so she enthusiastically offered up his name:
"When I came to Paris, I went to several fashion shows and found
Paris fashions pretty and sophisticated. But when I saw the collection
of Hubert de Givenchy, I felt he would make the clothes that most
suited me," she acknowledged. [19]

"WHEN I CAME TO PARIS, I WENT TO SEVERAL FASHION SHOWS AND FOUND PARIS FASHIONS PRETTY AND SOPHISTICATED"

AUDREY HEPBURN ON HUBERT DE GIVENCHY

The six-foot-six Givenchy, only a year older than Audrey, was from
a wealthy Beauvais family, who owned the Gobelins and Beauvais
tapestry factories. He studied drawing at the École Nationale
Supérieure des Beaux-Arts while training with couturier Jacques Fath,
who had been impressed by his portfolio of sketches. After working
as artistic director for Elsa Schiaparelli, at her headquarters on Place
Vendôme, his family helped to finance his new salon in a nineteenth-
century Gothic building on rue Alfred de Vigny, which he opened

in February 1952. His debut collection focused on separates, such as clean white ruffled blouses and white or black bodices worn with contrasting skirts or trousers. He hired three of the most popular Paris fashion models of the day – Capucine, Suzy Parker and Bettina Graziani – to showcase his designs and with these first collections, came to the attention of *Harper's Bazaar* editor Carmel Snow, who hailed him as "the new name to know". By 1954, the magazine was reporting that "his whole collection has real authority and technique, as well as ideas. Givenchy is now among the top designers."

In the summer of 1953, Paramount called Givenchy's salon, to make arrangements for a "Miss Hepburn" to visit. Like Balenciaga, the designer was also in the midst of preparing his latest collection, but assuming it was the actress Katharine Hepburn, and adoring her relaxed androgynous style, he agreed that she could select a number of outfits for the film.

The woman who walked through the door of his salon was very different from the one he was expecting. He described her as "this very thin person with beautiful eyes, short hair, thick eyebrows", dressed in Capri pants, a white T-shirt and ballet slippers, and with a gondolier's tourist straw hat branded with the word "Venezia", which she must have picked up on her travels. [20] He was disappointed to see it wasn't the great Hepburn, star of *The Philadelphia Story*, in front of him and explained to her he didn't have the time or the resources for a custom-made wardrobe. She offered to look through the rails and choose some pieces herself from his current collection. Audrey had an eye for what would complement her figure, emphasizing her supposed flaws, such as her defined collarbone and strong, slender arms, rather than covering them up. Givenchy's initial disappointment soon disappeared after they went for lunch together and her charm quickly won him over.

Hubert de Givenchy, photographed in
his atelier in the 1950s.

In anticipation of her arrival in Paris, Edith Head had given Audrey a list of the items that would be required for her costumes, as per the specifications of the script. She needed a dark travelling suit in navy or charcoal grey, a "very smart French day dress", some "extreme French hats" to wear with the suit, a couple of blouses and a ballgown that would be a real show-stopper. When she tried on the dresses in the salon, she exclaimed that they were "exactly what I need!" and they also proved to be an almost perfect fit for her. [21] Givenchy found that once she had slipped on the couture, like Sabrina, she transformed in front of his eyes, and that the "change from the little girl who arrived that morning was unbelievable." [22]

"WHAT USED TO BE CALLED A DÉCOLLETÉ BATEAU, AFTERWARD IT WAS CALLED THE DÉCOLLETÉ SABRINA."

HUBERT DE GIVENCHY ON THE ICONIC SABRINA COSTUME

The stunning silk organdie evening gown, which would be worn to the Larrabee ball, was based on Givenchy's two-piece "Inês De Castro" design for the 1953 spring/summer collection, but he switched the black spaghetti strap top to a strapless white organza bodice, which he felt was more suited for a summer ball. [23]

Audrey selected a wool double-breasted suit for her arrival back in Long Island from Paris. Director Billy Wilder described how the Glen Cove station scene was "a very important moment in the picture. We simply must sell the girl's transition. She must look delicious reappearing on Long Island." [24]

She also chose a black cocktail dress with a bateau neckline, which was a wide neckline with the straps secured with little bows.

Audrey wore a stunning ballgown selected from Givenchy, Paris, to film the summer party scene in *Sabrina*.

The black Givenchy cocktail
dress in *Sabrina* set trends with its
"bateau" neckline.

The dress would be created from a Givenchy sketch in Paramount's wardrobe department and was to become one of the most coveted of the film's costumes. Givenchy later said: "What used to be called a *décolleté bateau*, afterward it was called the *décolleté* Sabrina." [25]

After her first fittings at Givenchy's atelier in July 1953, the actress flew to Nice for the weekend, returning to Paris for a second fitting before travelling back to London, where she lived with her mother in an apartment in South Audley Street, Mayfair. The sketches and fabric samples were then airmailed to Edith Head and the completed garments followed later. Edith Head was able to design some of Audrey's costumes, not just Sabrina's "before" pinafore, but the slim black top, cigarette pants and ballet slippers. This was the youthful look of young Parisians on the Left Bank, shaped by the singer Juliette Gréco, who chose to dress all in black and would be a style eternally linked to Audrey in Paris. Sabrina, like the many American women who went to Paris in the early fifties, admired these countercultural existentialists who smoked Gauloises cigarettes at Café de Flore or Les Deux Magots in Saint-Germain-des-Prés, and listened to Edith Piaf, just as Sabrina hums "La Vie en Rose".

"This is what you do on your very first day in Paris," Sabrina (Audrey) tells Linus (Humphrey Bogart). "You get yourself some rain, not just a drizzle but honest-to-goodness rain. And then you find yourself someone really nice, drive her through the Bois de Boulogne in a taxi. The rain's very important because that's when Paris smells its sweetest. It's the damp chestnut trees, you see."

It was when she was in Paris in summer 1953, during those consultations with Givenchy, that Hepburn may have first seen *Lili*, a fantasy MGM musical that told the story of an orphan (Leslie Caron) and a carnival puppeteer, played by the American actor Mel Ferrer, who was, like Audrey, fluent in French. Audrey was so enchanted by the film that she went back to see it three times. The French-American

69

Caron would often be compared to her. Both were waifish and European, and their lives had many parallels; they were trained ballet dancers, they modelled a gamine haircut, and they would both play Gigi, with Caron later cast in the 1958 musical adaptation. The two "ingenues", who were competing against each other for the Best Actress Oscar in 1953 (for *Roman Holiday* and *Lili*) would meet on a number of occasions, at premieres and award shows. "She was reserved but very charming," Caron later reflected. [26]

Audrey had been so busy with her burgeoning career that she called off her wedding to James Hanson, knowing that she couldn't commit to being a wife when she was so busy with work. Hanson accepted her decision with grace, but there was another romance on the horizon. During the making of *Sabrina* she had fallen in love with the married William Holden; an affair doomed because he wouldn't, and couldn't, have any more children – a deal-breaker for Audrey. When Gregory Peck held a party in his London flat to celebrate the opening of *Roman Holiday* in August 1953, she met Mel Ferrer for the first time and was instantly captivated. After she completed work on *Sabrina*, Ferrer convinced her to make a return to Broadway for *Ondine* (1954), by the French playwright, Jean Giraudoux.

Ferrer was enamoured with Giraudoux's play after seeing it in Paris. A hit when first performed in the city in 1939, it was based on a German fairy tale about a water nymph who leaves her world to be with a chivalrous knight, and he falls under the spell of her magical beauty. Hepburn and Ferrer returned to Broadway to star in it together, with Mel playing the knight opposite Audrey's sprite. Audrey looked ravishing in her costume created by Valentina Schlee, with fishnet and fabric leaves designed to look like seaweed, and she received a rapturous reception for her performance.

With its black sweater, cigarette pants and
ballet slippers, Audrey's costume in *Sabrina*
defined bohemian Paris style.

At the same time as she was performing in *Ondine*, Audrey learned that she had been nominated for the Best Actress Oscar for *Roman Holiday*. Due to her commitments, she couldn't attend the Los Angeles ceremony in person, but she was ferried to Broadway's Century Theater, and when she was announced as the winner, she gave her speech in a white floral embroidered dress by Givenchy, which featured the bateau neckline that would be much-imitated after *Sabrina*. It was the first time that she was seen in public wearing his designs and it became one of the all-time classic Oscar looks. The same week that she collected her Oscar, Audrey was also the recipient of a Tony Award for *Ondine*. Only one other actress had won both an Oscar and a Tony in the same year (1952) – Shirley Booth for the film *Come Back, Little Sheba* and the play *The Time of the Cuckoo*.

The *New York Times* wrote in 1954: "Like Ondine, Miss Hepburn is half nymph, half Wunderkind, wholly herself. Unlike her, she had both feet planted firmly above sea level. Amid the rhinestone glare of the current glamour crop, she shines with the authenticity of a diamond." [27]

With so much triumph in such a short period of time, Audrey felt the pressure of expectation with *Sabrina*, to prove that her success in *Roman Holiday* wasn't just a stroke of luck. When released in September 1954, it was met with glowing reviews and audiences came out in droves to see the charming young star. The *New York Times'* Bosley Crowther described the magic of watching the film, where "the air was full of the tender and magical strains of La Vie en Rose." He described it as "the most delightful comedy-romance in years" and said that Audrey was "even more luminous as the daughter and pet of the servants' hall than she was as a princess last year, and no more than that can be said." [28]

Audrey chose to wear Givenchy to
collect her Best Actress Oscar for
Roman Holiday in 1954.

When even a jaded cinema critic can be charmed, it proved that the elegance of Paris had rubbed off on both Sabrina and the film itself. In autumn 1954, Hubert de Givenchy was also receiving rave reviews; *Harper's Bazaar* wrote that "his whole collection has real authority and technique, as well as ideas. Givenchy is now among the top designers."

Audrey received a second Oscar nomination as Best Actress for *Sabrina* and among the film's six nominations, Edith Head won for Best Costume Design. The studio had chosen not to give credit to Givenchy and when Head failed to mention him in her acceptance speech, he handled it with dignity. The acknowledgement would have been hugely beneficial to him this early in his career and Audrey, feeling the designer had been treated unjustly, vowed to make it up to him. From then on, she would choose Givenchy for her personal wardrobe and request him as a designer for her screen costumes.

"THE ROLE OF SABRINA FIRMLY ESTABLISHED AUDREY, AND HER STYLE, AS A SYMBOL OF EUROPEAN ELEGANCE."

Following the release of *Sabrina*, *Silver Screen* posed the question, "Is Hollywood shifting its accent on sex? She's changing Hollywood's taste in girls. From the full-bosomed, sweater-filling type with more curves than the New York Central Railroad, to the lean, umbrella-shaped variety." [29]

The role of Sabrina firmly established Audrey, and her style, as a symbol of European elegance. She had a Continental sensibility, often placed in the same category as Italian Pier Angeli, and even the French bombshell Brigitte Bardot. *McCall's* reporter Art Seidenbaum, who watched her on the set of *My Fair Lady*, said she was to haute couture "what Bardot is to bath towels".

Givenchy hired a model, Jacky Mazel, who closely resembled Audrey, to wear his couture around Paris.

Audrey was the new style icon for the fifties and Hubert de Givenchy experienced a wave of new customers at his Paris salon, as women sought to achieve the Hepburn magic for themselves. Givenchy hired a model, Jacky Mazel, who resembled Audrey and was photographed wearing his couture around Paris as she browsed the artist stalls in Montmartre and sat at outdoor pavement cafés.

As much as she found reassurance in his designs, Audrey would inspire Givenchy's future collections. She loved the comfort and simplicity of his clothing, in those monochrome tones she felt suited her so well: black, white, navy, beige and pale pink. Givenchy called her "the perfect model". He said, "I'm always inspired by Miss Hepburn when I look for my own mannequins. She has the ideal face and figure, with her long, slim body and swanlike neck. It's a real pleasure to make clothes for her." [30]

In 1954, following two years of living nomadically, Audrey was asked in a radio interview where she would like to settle: "If I had my choice, and if I had the money, I'd have an apartment in London, an apartment in New York, and someplace in the country – providing, of course, I could travel a lot and go to Paris and Rome a great deal! But of course, the day I marry a man I'm very much in love with, and he lives in Timbuktu, that's where I'll live." [31]

She chose to base herself in the Swiss village of Bürgenstock, overlooking Lake Lucerne, where she found the views of the Alps to be soothing after her hectic schedule of the past few years. It was here, in a little chapel, that she and Mel Ferrer married in September 1954. Despite her devotion to Givenchy, for her wedding dress she selected another French designer, Pierre Balmain, who created a romantic, tea-length organdie gown, worn with a crown of white roses. Balmain, an apprentice to Molyneux and Lucien Lelong, had

Audrey in Paris in 1954, wearing a white
lace dress designed by Givenchy.

opened his fashion house in Paris in 1945 and with his romantic silhouettes came to represent the post-war fashion revival in the city.

Now that she was married, Audrey placed her career second to being a wife. She chose not to make more than two films a year, sometimes with long breaks between them, and vowed to be away from her husband as little as possible. At this period in her life, Audrey was traditional in her view of marriage: "It's so nice being a wife and having your husband take over your worries for you," she said. "American women have a tendency to take over too much, and in that way, they miss out on a lot of fun that their European sisters have." [32] She had been desperate to start a family, but in March 1955 suffered a devastating miscarriage. It was a traumatic event that she admitted was one of the most painful experiences of her life, and left her inconsolable for a time.

After a break from work, she and her husband travelled to Rome in June 1955 to star in the big budget *War and Peace* (1956), filmed at Cinecittà Studios. With Mel Ferrer cast as Prince Andrei, Audrey agreed to play Natasha Rostova for a salary of $350,000 plus expenses – the highest fee for any actress in the world at this time. It was only her third Hollywood movie and the modest Hepburn couldn't help but feel that the huge salary was undeserved: "I'm not worth it!" she told her agent, Kurt Frings, as he negotiated the contract.

Being an historical epic, it wasn't possible for Givenchy to create her costumes and this version of Audrey on screen was different – her signature short hair was gone in favour of long tresses to suit the period timeframe. After *War and Peace*, which she said "felt like endlessly dressing up for the opera", she wanted to do something light-hearted, with lashings of glamour, and what came along was *Funny Face* and then *Love in the Afternoon*.

79

Following the release of *Sabrina* (1954), Audrey was greeted warmly by fans in Paris.

CHAPTER FOUR

Bonjour, Paris!

WITH PARISIAN STREETSCAPES IN GLORIOUS
TECHNICOLOR, A COVETABLE WARDROBE
BY HUBERT DE GIVENCHY, AND AUDREY
HEPBURN AND FRED ASTAIRE DANCING
TO A GERSHWIN SCORE, *FUNNY FACE*,
DIRECTED BY STANLEY DONEN, HAD ALL
THE INGREDIENTS TO BE THE ULTIMATE FILM
ABOUT THE WORLD'S FASHION CAPITAL.

Originally to be called *Wedding Day*, it was based on an unproduced play by Leonard Gershe, inspired by the life of his friend, fashion photographer Richard Avedon. After producer Roger Edens bought the rights, he combined it with the Gershwin score from *Funny Face*, a 1927 stage musical originally starring Astaire and his sister Adele. Avedon was hired as visual and colour consultant and he shot the fashion stills of Audrey used in the film, showcasing the flamboyant artistry that he was famed for. In another nod to the fashion industry, 1950s supermodels Dovima and Suzy Parker featured in cameo roles.

The script offered a further twist on the Cinderella storyline of *Sabrina*, with Audrey this time playing a Greenwich Village bookworm, Jo Stockton, who is discovered by a Richard Avedon-esque photographer, Dick Avery (Fred Astaire), and taken to Paris to be the new face of *Quality* fashion magazine. In keeping with the Pygmalion themes, she feels unappreciated by her mentor and he at first fails to acknowledge what makes her so special. Audrey was 27 during filming, but her innocent appearance allowed her to play a girl who was supposed to be a few years younger than her real age.

Quality's editor Maggie Prescott (Kay Thompson) is a woman who sells consumerist dreams through her magazine, but "wouldn't be caught dead" in the pink clothes she's been telling her customers to buy. When she and her assistants sail into Jo's bookstore to do a fashion shoot, Jo is horrified at the mess they make. Despite her protests that she doesn't approve of fashion magazines and that it's just "silly dresses on silly women", Jo longs to go to Paris as it's the home of the intellectual "Empathicalism" movement, which she admires so much.

"You'd have a ball," Dick tells her. "You'd go to a party every night, drink nothing but champagne, swim in perfume and have a new love affair every hour on the hour."

"If I went to Paris, it would be to go to Emile Flostre's lectures ...

Audrey on the steps of the Louvre, mimicking
the "Winged Victory of Samothrace" statue,
in *Funny Face*.

PREVIOUS Kay Thompson, Fred Astaire and
Audrey filming the "Bonjour Paris" musical
number for *Funny Face* (1957).

the greatest living philosopher," she says seriously. Once he leaves, she dances with a brightly coloured hat, left behind from the fashion shoot. It's as if a little bit of its magic can rub off on her as it glows amid the drab surroundings of the bookstore and it might help transport her to Paris. When Dick persuades Jo that she could be the new, and unconventional, face of *Quality* magazine, she only agrees as a means of getting to Paris, where she hopes to explore the intellectual highlights of the city. When she fails to turn up for her dress fittings and make-up, he knows exactly where to find her: in the Hollywood cliché of the Left Bank, with cyclists wearing berets and couples kissing in dark recesses, and where Jo is listening to jazz and poetry recitals in a cave club.

As well as the fashion industry, *Funny Face* was a send-up of the Left Bank Existentialists and America's Beat generation – a movement soon to be co-opted by the capitalist world of advertising, the exact same thing they were railing against. Audrey, as the representative of the youthful femininity of that era, was transformed into the ultimate beatnik, wearing a black turtleneck and cigarette pants as she throws her body into avant-garde shapes in the smoke-filled club.

In New York, Greenwich Village was the heart of this alternative literary movement, but its ideals were born in the street cafés and cellars of the Left Bank, with the Café de Flore considered the birthplace. It was where Jean-Paul Sartre and Simone de Beauvoir, the figureheads of Existentialism, had held court, and where singer and actress Juliette Gréco, in her black turtlenecks and bulky coats, had become a style icon.

Existentialism was a philosophy that questioned existence. It stepped into the space of religion, where it offered freedom of expression, of simply "being" and embracing jazz music, poetry, pulp fiction and sexual experimentation. The novels of Sartre and de Beauvoir were the topics of conversation in newspapers and on the streets of post-war Paris, with Sartre's *L'Être et le Néant* (Being and Nothingness) the must-read work that sparked a movement.

Audrey in the bar of the Hotel Raphaël, her
favourite place to stay in Paris.

By the fifties, the Left Bank, or more particularly, Saint-Germain-des-Prés, had earned a reputation for being a fashionably cheap area where writers and artists could meet and talk over coffee or wine, or visit the cave nightclubs to listen to jazz, much like the areas of Soho, in London, and New York City's Greenwich Village. In those days, there were plenty of affordable apartments and hotels packed into the narrow streets that opened out onto leafy courtyards or offered glimpses of the Seine, with the booksellers hawking old books and magazines from their riverside boxes. It was youthful, exciting and artistic, where ethnic communities mixed with the students from the Sorbonne and the École des Beaux-Arts.

By 1956 Audrey was established as one of Hollywood's biggest stars and she had her pick of the top directors, screenwriters and co-stars. She possessed the clout to command a $150,000 salary, a

"BY 1956 AUDREY WAS ESTABLISHED AS ONE OF HOLLYWOOD'S BIGGEST STARS"

87

luxury hotel suite at the Hotel Raphaël and the Givenchy wardrobe, which she would be able to keep after production was completed as part of her contract. She insisted on *Funny Face* being shot in Paris so that she could be in the same city as her husband while he was shooting the Jean Renoir comedy *Elena et Les Hommes* (1956) with Ingrid Bergman. The Billy Wilder film, *Love in the Afternoon*, which Audrey was supposed to be filming in Paris first, had been delayed due to timings in the production, and so the musical had stepped into this space in the meantime. *Funny Face* was set to be her first screen

Taking a break during the filming of the "Bonjour Paris" number, with co-star Fred Astaire in the background.

OVERLEAF Audrey with Fred Astaire as she signs autographs at the Eiffel Tower, during the making of *Funny Face*.

musical and she was both excited and terrified of starring opposite and dancing with Fred Astaire, who, as her love interest, was double her age at 57. Audrey later confessed that on meeting him for the first time, she was "so shaken that I threw up my breakfast". [33] According to director Stanley Donen, "they loved each other, they got on splendidly. He admired her and respected her and was charmed by her...and she was absolutely in awe of his talent." [34]To prepare for dancing with such a legend, she spent three months refreshing her ballet skills at the Paris Opera Ballet, with lessons from dance master Lucien Legrand. Her dance training coincided with Paris's coldest winter in years, and while Legrand wore three sweaters to keep warm in the sub-zero temperature of the studio, Audrey arrived in her black leotard, and insisted she receive no special treatment.

Because of the seasonal nature of preparing his Paris collections, Hubert de Givenchy was only available to design for the film in autumn 1955 or spring 1956, but producer Harry Caplan raved that the designer was "young, enthusiastic and full of ideas" and a deal was offered for 13 complete outfits for Audrey and gowns for around 65 models, for 17.5 million French francs. It was a huge commission for Givenchy, and after designing the costumes in Paris, they were then created in the Paramount Pictures workrooms in Hollywood, with fabric sourced in France.

As Paramount's head designer, Edith Head expected to be in charge of costumes for all of the studio's top stars. Audrey Hepburn had already disappointed her during the making of *Sabrina* when she requested Hubert de Givenchy for the post-Paris makeover. But Edith had to be used in some capacity in *Funny Face* as "she was built into the contract" Donen told *Vanity Fair.* "I would have liked Givenchy to do the whole picture ... if you do a picture about high fashion, you can't have Edith Head." [35]

91

A series of images during the filming of a fashion shoot at the Gare du Nord, Paris, for *Funny Face.*

Audrey and Mel were greeted by young
ballerinas from the Paris Opera at Orly
Airport to begin the filming of *Funny Face*.

Instead, she created the drab "before" costumes for Audrey, the smart outfits for the staff at *Quality* magazine, including the "Think Pink" sequence, and Kay Thompson's wardrobe. Thompson plays the *Quality* magazine editor with panache and cynical humour. She was based on *Harper's Bazaar*'s iconic editors Carmel Snow and Diana Vreeland, who both loved Paris. Indeed Thompson was so taken with her time filming *Funny Face* that she was inspired to write her successful children's book, *Eloise in Paris*, published in 1957. Yet she was unhappy at not being assigned a real couturier to dress her and insisted on having at least one Givenchy piece. She felt Edith's safe signature suits were too conventional for a character like Diana Vreeland, who had real fashion flair. As a compromise, Givenchy designed the camel-hair coat for the "Bonjour, Paris!" sequence.

Interiors were shot at Paramount Pictures' Hollywood studio in April 1956 before the production moved to Paris for location shooting. The schedule would take in all of the city's major landmarks – the Louvre, Eiffel Tower, the baroque interior of the Palais Garnier opera house, Notre-Dame cathedral and the banks of the Seine, Montmartre and the Jardin des Tuileries. They formed a majestic backdrop to Audrey in Givenchy's gowns, which put Technicolor to brilliant effect with their joyous colour. Her costumes included a white satin evening dress with pink velvet stole (her "Cinderella-at-the ball" moment), a black-and-white lace bouffant evening gown, a sapphire taffeta cape and gloves, a sunny yellow satin evening gown and a strapless red evening dress.

Audrey flew into the city with her husband Mel Ferrer on May 23, 1956, checking into room 402 of the Hotel Raphaël with 50 pieces of luggage and the film's key costume, the wedding dress, in her possession. The entire sixth floor of the hotel would be taken up with the wardrobe, hairdressing and make-up departments, allowing the actress to be changed and made up in the comfort of the hotel before doing location shooting.

The Art Deco Hotel Raphaël was located on 17 Avenue Kleber, not far from the Champs-Élysées. It featured a private terrace with panoramic views over Paris's rooftops to the Eiffel Tower, where Audrey could relax with a whisky after a long day's filming. The hotel was constructed in the 1920s, when avant-garde artists and bohemian writers filled the city with creativity. The hotel, named after the Italian Renaissance artist, was designed as a tribute to the arts, with its black-and-white checked lobby and plush red velvet and wood-panelled bar. It had become a favourite for the Hollywood set, with Ava Gardner, Grace Kelly, Katharine Hepburn and Henry Fonda all having stayed in its classically French palatial rooms.

Audrey tended to be a homebody and so she decorated her suite with her own comforts, packing in her suitcases her white bed and table linens, white sets of china, a candelabra, two knitted blankets, tiny Limoges ashtrays and cigarette boxes and her favourite pictures and books. "Home is wherever Mel and I create it, wherever our work takes us – Paris, California, before that Italy, and next Mexico. We move our

"HOME IS WHEREVER MEL AND I CREATE IT"

home with us, like snails," she told a reporter for *Voice of America* in 1956. [36] She brought little bits of familiarity with her to elegant suites in luxury hotels as she wanted this comfort of home to fill the space while she hoped she could have a child.

Audrey and Mel also ensured they travelled with a phonograph and records to play jazz in their suite in the evenings. "I like jazz best now," she said. "It makes me want to move. But I was stiff as a poker as a jazz dancer, always off beat on the simplest syncopation." [37]

One evening the couple threw a dinner party for cast and crew at a romantic restaurant with beautiful views to Montmartre and Ingrid Bergman, who was staying at the Raphaël while acting opposite Mel in *Elena et Les Hommes*, was invited too. When Audrey discovered

Brightening up the gloomy weather
during a scene at the Arc de Triomphe du
Carrousel (*Funny Face*).

that it was the Unit Production Manager's birthday, she asked the kitchen if they could make a cake, and led the guests, including Bergman, into singing "happy birthday". The Ferrers also dined with Jean Renoir at some of the city's best restaurants, including Maxim's and Lasserre.

At a press lunch on the second floor of the Eiffel Tower to launch the location shooting, Audrey felt under siege from popping flashbulbs. "Now and then it staggers you," she reflected on her immense fame. "So many people pointing cameras, especially in Europe. Now and then, you find yourself out of your depth. The questions – all the way from what do I think of love or how does it feel to be a star, to enormous ones, even political, with as many prongs as a pitchfork." [38]

Audrey may have felt overwhelmed by the fame, but she still remained humble and unfailingly polite. A reporter from *Photoplay* magazine recounted a moment during the filming of the "Bonjour Paris" number at the Eiffel Tower, when the cast and crew were taking a break on the second floor of the landmark. They were seated around a long table for lunch, when Donen's wife, Marion Marshall, walked into the room carrying their baby. Donen rose quickly, looking for another chair. It was Audrey who quietly sprung to her feet, sourced the spare chair and carried it over to Marion. [39]

Typically, Paris in the spring and early summer was bright and balmy, but in 1956 it was a "symphony of pouring rain and cold winds", when Paramount's production crew arrived. On April 16, producers noted in a memo, "Paris is still having a morning frost and some of the plants are dead. Trees were not in foliage and it too is a dreary site."[40]

As the *New York Times* reported: "Song lyrics in *Funny Face* compliment Paris as the city of sunshine and happiness. Faced with downpours and umbrellas sprouting all over town, a line was thrown in during a scene at Orly airport on how unseasonable the weather was in Paris." Audrey took advantage of delays in filming caused by the bad weather by going to the studios of the Paris Opéra Ballet to refresh her choreography.[41]

Audrey at the Palais Garnier, home of the
Paris Opera, wearing a dramatic emerald
evening coat designed by Givenchy.

Taking a break during the filming of
Funny Face, with a view over Paris
from Montmartre.

One of the fashion montages was filmed outside the Tuileries Palace during a downpour and colourful balloons were brought in to help lift the scene out of the gloominess. The next day, Stanley Donen had to hire firefighters to use their hoses to simulate rain in the Jardin des Tuileries so that there would be continuity in the footage from the previous day. There were other contentious issues. For example, 100,000 francs was donated to the Château de Versailles fund for filming as they objected to heavy equipment being taken onto the roof of the palace for location shots. Scenes in congested areas, such as Place de L'Opéra, La Madeleine and Arc de Triomphe de l'Étoile, all had to be filmed on Sundays so as not to disrupt traffic, while others, like the Louvre, could only be filmed at night.

With crowds rushing to catch a glimpse of the movie stars, the decision was made to do some of the location shoots at dawn to capture the city at its quietest, such as filming the sequence at the Paris Opera at 5 a.m. Despite this early hour, Audrey and Fred Astaire still became tourist attractions in their own right and fans who were up before sunrise were treated to a glimpse of the production.

Production manager Kenneth Deland told the press: "If it rains lightly, we won't stop. Paris frequently looks even lovelier in the rain. This is a calculated risk we have to take. Our schedule is as tight as a drum. We have worked it out on a minute-to-minute basis otherwise, moving from the part of Paris that looks loveliest in the morning to locations that look best at twilight, and in the evening to those that are most dramatic at night."

When it was discovered that the Trocadero fountain was without water as it was under repair, production crew used a hose to fill the basin with water themselves in order to complete a particular set piece. According to a May 28, 1956 injury report, Audrey slipped and fell as she ran on the wet ground while filming by the fountain. The assistant director then sprained a ligament in his leg as he ran to assist her. Slips aside, she joked that she was lucky not to fall down the steps of the Louvre when asked to repeatedly run down them for one of the

Funny Face featured a fashion shoot at
the fountains in the Parc du Château
de Versailles.

fashion shoots. As part of the film, the real Richard Avedon was tasked with taking the still photographs of Audrey in Givenchy's spectacular gowns. She stands in front of the Arc de Triomphe du Carrousel in a black dress, a bunch of colourful balloons in hand; she runs down the steps of the Louvre in a long red gown, mimicking the Winged Victory of Samothrace statue as she holds a red veil aloft; she wears a jewel-green coat at the steps of Place de l'Opéra, and on a Gare du Nord platform, in a taupe wool suit, she is immersed in a cloud of steam from the Flèche d'Or luxury train, as if from the pages of *Anna Karenina*.

Audrey had first been photographed by Avedon on arrival in New York when she starred in *Gigi*, and then for the April 1956 cover of *Harper's Bazaar* and she felt truly comfortable posing for him. Later, she said: "For Richard, I've happily swung through swings, stood in clouds of steam, been drenched with rain, and descended endless flights of stairs without

"THE 'BONJOUR, PARIS!' SEQUENCE OFFERS A FASCINATING GLIMPSE OF THE PARIS OF THE FIFTIES"

looking and without breaking my neck... Only with Richard have I been able to shed my innate self-consciousness in front of the camera." [42]

One of the most celebrated scenes is where Audrey joyfully dances to jazz in a subterranean Left Bank café. She wears a black turtleneck, black trousers and black ballet slippers as inspired by the Existentialist movement, but this scene was earlier filmed, along with the other interiors, on Paramount's backlot in Hollywood.

The "Bonjour, Paris!" number offers a fascinating glimpse of the Paris of the fifties, as the sequence follows Audrey, Astaire and Kay Thompson as they gaze out of the window of the plane as it flies over the city's famous sights, from the Eiffel Tower to the Champs-Élysées. On arrival at the airport, each agrees that they are above the usual attractions, but they then explore the city on their own. They are photographed embracing its striking, and familiar, landmarks in amazement that they're actually here, sometimes using a split screen, until they are surprised to meet up on the viewing platform of the Eiffel Tower – as they had all rejected it for being too "touristy".

Stanley Donen held back filming this key musical number in the hopes of capturing some sunshine. Eventually it was filmed on June 14, with umbrellas and raincoats now used as props. The scene depicted the simple pleasures in discovering the city, with Fred Astaire strolling down the Champs-Élysées, Audrey enjoying Montmartre, Kay Thompson by the Seine, with black clouds looming over Notre-Dame and the trio celebrating their arrival at the Eiffel Tower.

With the rain continuing for weeks, they couldn't hold off filming the wedding dance scene any longer. It was to take place on a little island in the gardens of the Château de la Reine Blanche in Chantilly, 25 miles from Paris, and they arrived to find the ground sodden and muddy. The actors' feet were sinking ankle-deep into the bog, destroying Audrey's white satin dancing shoes. "It was like dancing on glue," Donen told the BBC. "It was like dancing in the water and if you look at the film, you can see Audrey's shoes – in spite of the fact that they're very low heels, they still go into the full depth of the mud." [43]

He recalled that Fred Astaire was getting "very crotchety" and demanded that he fix it – "I don't care! Put down a wood floor and paint it green." Everyone was tense until Audrey suddenly quipped, "Here I've been waiting 20 years to dance with Fred Astaire and what do I get? Mud in my eye!"

Work on *Funny Face* ended in the first week of July 1956 and the Billy Wilder film, *Love in the Afternoon*, was ready to start shooting almost immediately. After a long weekend in London to see friends, and a brief period of relaxation in Bürgenstock, it was time for Audrey to report back to Paris.

Audrey and Fred Astaire rehearsing their romantic dance number in the grounds of the Château de la Reine Blanche, Paris.

CHAPTER FIVE

A City for Lovers

FOR YOUNG VISITORS TO PARIS IN THE
1950S, THERE WAS NOTHING MORE
ROMANTIC THAN STAYING IN A GARRET
ROOM, LOCATED IN THE ATTIC SPACE
OF THE CITY'S NINETEENTH-CENTURY
LIMESTONE AND WROUGHT-IRON BALCONY
APARTMENT BLOCKS.

These had been constructed as part of the regeneration of the city by Napoleon III and his right-hand man, Georges-Eugène Haussmann, who helped transform Paris into the City of Light. Accessed up numerous flights of stairs to reach the eaves of the building, they had originally been created as maid quarters, or *chambres à bonnes*. With their sloping ceilings and little windows, which offered expansive views over the city, they were, by the late 1940s, considered the epitome of bohemian living.

In her memoirs of being a young American in 1950s Paris, Beverley Lehman West wrote of her joy at living in a top floor garret on the Left Bank of Paris. It had a slanted ceiling, like the garrets in operas *La Traviata* and *La Bohème*, and, she said: "I could look out over half the city. The toilet room and running water tap were in the hall, to be shared with the other tenants. This floor had been inhabited by servants in these chambres à bonnes, but now housed artists and would-be writers." [44]

Love in the Afternoon tapped into this sense of romance as it begins with a view over the Paris rooftops to the Eiffel Tower, from the window of an attic apartment. This clearly sets out its intention from the very beginning: it will be a love letter to the most amorous of cities.

"In Paris, people eat better. In Paris, people make love," says Claude Chavasse (Maurice Chevalier) in the opening sequence voiceover. "Well, perhaps not better, but certainly more often. They do it anytime, any place. On the Left Bank, on the Right Bank, and in between ... Poodles do it, tourists do it, generals do it, once in a while even existentialists do it. There is young love, and old love. Married love, and illicit love."

The story begins in the Place Vendôme, outside The Ritz, as a private detective spies in its windows from the top of the Napoleon I column. The camera then pans to suite 14, occupied by a wealthy

PREVIOUS Sam Shaw photographed Audrey
on the streets of Paris during the making of
Love in the Afternoon (1957).

Audrey with co-star Gary Cooper in the
corridors of The Ritz Paris, during the making
of *Love in the Afternoon.*

Arriving at The Ritz Paris on Place
Vendôme in 1955.

OVERLEAF Audrey and Mel on a
country road outside of Paris in 1956.

American lothario, Frank Flannigan (Gary Cooper). The private detective is Claude Chavasse (Chevalier) and he lives at Number 17, rue Malebranche, with his cello-playing daughter Ariane Chavasse, played by Audrey. They live in one of those romantic Parisian apartments, set behind huge double doors, which when opened up reveals an eclectic, bohemian world. While her father is investigating Flannigan, Ariane becomes fascinated by the stories of his affairs and hunts him down in the Ritz hotel, where she sets out to experience his seduction technique for herself.

Mel Ferrer's acting career was predominantly based in France and Italy and after being cast in Jean Renoir's *Elena et les Hommes*, filmed in Paris, Audrey had requested her next film also be made on location in Paris. Such was her value as a star that Paramount producers were willing to do what they could to ensure the couple could be together and so they chose the novel *Ariane*, by Claude Anet, as a basis for her next movie. Retitled *Love in the Afternoon*, it was to be directed by Billy Wilder, who had so sensitively captured Audrey in *Sabrina*, and with Gary Cooper as her much-older love interest. With the production delayed, *Funny Face* stepped into this slot and once filming was completed on the musical in July 1956, she only had a short break in Bürgenstock before flying back to Paris to begin work on the Billy Wilder film.

As with *Sabrina*, *Love in the Afternoon* deals with a young woman who lusts after an older, and unsuitable, man. Audrey's characters possess an innocence and naivety, but like all fairy tales, there is a dark side. In *Sabrina*, her character is suffering so badly that she wants to die rather than go to Paris and attempts suicide by turning on the engines of all the cars in the garage. It's a bleak moment, even if this scene is treated humorously. Audrey was protective of her screen persona, preferring to exist in a space that was softer and gentler than reality. This would be evident in *Breakfast at Tiffany's*,

where the money Holly Golightly receives from men for her company is under the guise of something quirkier.

Like *Sabrina*, Ariane feels a deep, painful longing for this more sophisticated older man and she regularly sneaks off to the Ritz to visit his luxurious room, where she pretends she's much worldlier than she really is. Audrey had been paired with older men in *Sabrina* and *Funny Face*, but the age gap in *Love in the Afternoon* appears more pronounced, particularly as her character is a naïve student, and it is a lustier relationship than the chaste bonds with Humphrey Bogart and Fred Astaire. Cary Grant was Wilder's first choice, but he was unavailable and he also felt that at 52, he was too old for 27-year-old Audrey Hepburn. Ariane uses her innocence against Cooper, so it becomes "Red Riding Hood gobbling up the wolf", as one critic said.

The last scene of *Love in the Afternoon* is set at Gare de Lyon, as Gary Cooper is about to board the train for the Riviera. Ariane, her heart clearly breaking, pretends she doesn't care. As the train pulls away, she continues to walk, and then run, alongside it, not yet able to say farewell. "Goodbye, thin girl," he says. The train moves faster and she still runs alongside. Then he sweeps down and scoops her into his arms and into his train carriage.

This ending proved controversial; they embrace in his private compartment, but with concern in the more conservative US as to what would happen on this overnight journey outside of wedlock, there was a final title which made clear they were soon to be married.

Audrey was quick to defend the age gap with Cooper. "The charge is particularly unfair to Coop," she said. "In *Love in the Afternoon* he's not trying to fool anyone. He's supposed to be a man of 50 – that's the whole point of the story."[45] As well as being close with Cooper, she also charmed Maurice Chevalier, who wrote her a telegram on the

Givenchy designed a series of delicate gowns for Audrey as a cello player in *Love in the Afternoon.*

During location filming at the Château de
Vitry at Gambais, Audrey brought her mother,
Baroness Ella van Heemstra.

first day of filming: "How proud I would be, and full of love I would be, if I really had a daughter like you."

Love in the Afternoon was the second film in a row where Audrey's costumes were designed by Hubert de Givenchy and this time, audiences were expected to suspend their belief that a young music student would be able to afford these pieces. But their elegant simplicity suited her perfectly and meant that it didn't really matter. Even when she's scaling the outside of the Ritz, it seemed right for her to be wearing a black cocktail dress while doing so. Givenchy's costumes helped give her confidence in her performance and as she said in 1956, "His are the only clothes in which I am myself."

Givenchy would later say of the woman he counted as one of his closest friends: "She had an elegance, she knew how to walk, she knew what she wanted, she knew the faults in her face, she knew

"HIS ARE THE ONLY CLOTHES IN WHICH I AM MYSELF."

AUDREY HEPBURN ON FRENCH DESIGNER HUBERT DE GIVENCHY

herself perfectly. She was true, honest. From time to time I'd say, because she was so thin, 'Wouldn't it be better if we didn't show your collarbone?' And she'd say, 'No, it doesn't bother me.' As Billy Wilder said, 'What counts in Audrey is her allure.' And she was kind. When the telephone would ring in the studio, I knew when it was her. I would answer and she'd say, 'I know you are busy, but I want to send you a big kiss,' and she'd hang up. *That* was Audrey." [46]

Audrey adored the "delicate, romantic quality" of Givenchy and the costumes he created were light and fresh, to suit the persona of her character, Ariane, even if they were far more luxurious than she could have afforded in reality. With a budget of $35,000 (equivalent to over $380,000 today) they possessed the 1950s silhouette with full, tea-length skirts and fitted bodices, and embellishments such as bows, lace and embroidered flowers. There was the tasteful black silk cocktail dress for her visit to the Ritz, with its skirt of box pleats inspired by the cello she plays.

For a trip to the opera house, she wears a white tulle ballet-style dress edged with silver-threaded lace and with a turquoise ribbon at the waist. Also included in the wardrobe was a floral embroidered afternoon dress, a grey and white tweed dress and a pair of slacks, a cotton blouse and a cardigan for the picnic scene. As the *Journal News* said, the fashions were "simplicity and youthfulness she most admires, combined with a touch of Paris sophistication." [47]

One of the looks that became a trend was the twice-tied silk scarf worn around Ariane's neck and over her head in the final scene. As one newspaper wrote at the time: "From the royal box at Wimbledon to the beaches of Cape Cod, women tied on scarves, hoping to achieve the same wistful, limpid-eye beauty of the heroine on the screen." [48] This youthful air was further enhanced by an updated hairstyle by her hairdresser Grazia de Rossi: a soft, jaw-length pageboy, which was centre-parted – "I thought people might have got tired seeing me in the old style," Audrey explained. "Now I have decided to keep this new look, even off the set." [49]

Like her previous films set in Paris, the city was a vital part of the story, and to capture the real qualities of it, Billy Wilder uprooted production and brought it to France. Filming took place at the Studios de Boulogne, France's largest film studio at the time, which was located in an old aircraft cabin factory in the Boulogne-Billancourt suburb, to the west of Paris. With heavy vehicle traffic a problem in Paris, Wilder decided he could save time by selecting his location sites and then choosing the designs for his interiors to be constructed at the Studios de Boulogne.

Cinematographer William Mellor and art director Alexandre Trauner spent a couple of weeks driving around Paris to find suitable locations. They ended up with 5,000 photographs and watercolours of the city streets, suburbs and hotel interiors. From these, Wilder

The delicate tulle ballet-style dress
worn to the Paris Opera.

selected the Bois de Boulogne, Montparnasse, where the Chavasse apartment is located on rue Malebranche, the Gare de Lyon for the final scene, the Place Vendôme and the Ritz.

The grand opera building, Palais Garnier, with its opulent gilt auditorium, was also an important location in the film. It's here that Ariane sees the opera *Tristan and Isolde*, about the illicit love between an Irish princess and a Cornish knight, and which had also made an appearance in *Funny Face*. From her balcony in the auditorium, she spies on Frank Flannagan seated in the stalls and then, after the show, hopes he'll notice her in her stunning opera dress. At first he doesn't recognise her, only referring to her as the "Thin Girl", but in this moment she charms him into pursuing her for another date.

Rather than filming in the corridors and rooms of the Ritz, which would have been humming with guests, a luxury suite was replicated in painstaking detail on the sound stage, and which was enhanced by William Mellor's lighting. Mellor found working in Paris challenging, particularly as he didn't speak French, and without the expertise of his veteran sound stage assistants of Hollywood. He tended to light the sets himself and chose a low-key pattern from overhead to simulate the natural light from the chandeliers and the soft light and shadow from side lamps placed around the room. The auditorium of the Paris opera was also built on the sound stage and due to its immense size, was recreated in perspective, with flats and cardboard cut-outs. Even the imposing and ornate chandelier was a pasteboard replica. [50]

For the romantic picnic sequence, where Frank tries to woo Ariane with a serenade from his band of musicians and a flow of champagne, the production company moved three buses, seven trucks of camera and lighting equipment and 15 carloads of cast and crew to the

Ariane scales the walls of The Ritz
Paris in a black Givenchy dress.

Château de Vitry at Gambais. It was located 40 miles from Paris and featured twin lakes and idyllic woodland.

The weather and light conditions were unpredictable, with an hour of sunshine and then long stretches of cloudy sky. To ensure a full shooting day, Billy Wilder also transported two interior sets from the Studios de Boulogne – a Paris café and a hospital room – alongside a powerful generator and lighting equipment, and these were reconstructed in the Gambais woods and used for filming when the overcast sky prevented exterior photography.

Audrey brought her mother, the baroness, with her on location, and during her downtime, she took part in a photo shoot with American photojournalist Sam Shaw. Wearing the red cardigan and striped Troubadour pants of the picnic scene, he captured her in various locations by the lake and woods, sitting on the grassy bank and with a fishing net over her shoulder. Shaw, who shot the iconic series

"THE MOST INTRIGUINGLY CHILDISH ADULT, FEMININE TOMBOY I'VE EVER PHOTOGRAPHED ... SHE'S MANY WOMEN WRAPPED UP IN ONE."

PHOTOJOURNALIST SAM SHAW ON AUDREY HEPBURN

of photographs of Marilyn Monroe with her white skirts billowing up around her during the making of Wilder's *The Seven Year Itch* (1955), also took natural images of Audrey around Paris. Wearing her Givenchy costumes, and with her hair in the pageboy style, she was pictured in the woods of Bois de Boulogne, at a busy café counter and on grand Parisian street corners. He described her as "the most intriguingly childish adult, feminine tomboy I've ever photographed ... She's many women wrapped up in one." [51]

While filming in Paris, Audrey was once again staying at the Hotel Raphaël, but this time she was there without her husband as Mel was in the South of France making an MGM thriller, *The Vintage* (1957), with the Italian actress Pier Angeli.

Audrey photographed by Sam Shaw in the
grounds of the Château de Vitry at Gambais.

Margaret Gardner, a freelance writer, visited Audrey's hotel suite and noticed that it had been transformed into a space filled with her belongings. She had removed the hotel's furniture and instead the room had been decorated with her own pieces, along with rugs and table lamps, bedlinen and cushions, even her own drinks service. Whenever Audrey stayed in hotels, she wanted to make sure they had the comfortable familiarity of home. Her life was transient, so she needed that reassurance and found it with beloved pieces from her own life.

Even with her possessions around her in the suite at the Hotel Raphaël, she felt lonely. Just before he went to the South of France for filming, Mel bought his wife a Yorkshire terrier and she named him "Famous". He would become a much-loved companion as she took him for walks around the city and he kept her occupied in her studio dressing room. She was also busy with daily lessons on how to mimic the finger movements for playing the cello, which her character is either practising on or lugging around with her.

Every other weekend she would travel to the Riviera to see Mel and they would check into the Hotel du Cap-Eden-Roc, where they spent time swimming, playing tennis and exploring the countryside. On alternate weekends, he would come to Paris and they tried to move around the city as incognito as possible. They were spotted strolling along the Champs-Élysées one Sunday in September 1956, with their chauffeur-driven car following them at a discreet distance. In the evenings they would meet for drinks and dinner with Gary Cooper and director Billy Wilder and his wife, Audrey, choosing to dine in the luxury restaurants or the quiet bistros where they would be less likely to be spotted.

"We are very much in love," she told an *Evening Standard* reporter who visited the *Love in the Afternoon* set. "And I believe you have to work at that. I won't let my work affect my marriage. In our business, one is bound to be separated sometimes. At least we are still in the same country. One Sunday I go to see Mel in St Tropez, the next Sunday he comes to see me here. We phone each other every night." [52]

Audrey and Mel were together in Paris to celebrate his birthday at the end of August 1956 and Billy Wilder hosted a dinner in Mel's honour on the set at the studio, with Gary Cooper and Maurice Chevalier as special guests.

Despite the Hollywood depictions of Paris as a wonderland, the reality was somewhat different, with the continued worker strikes bringing the city to a halt, and with a number of political crises that impacted on its stability. Violence broke out across the city in late 1956, with protests following the Russian invasion of Hungary, the unrest around the Suez Canal crisis and over the next few years there were

"DESPITE THE HOLLYWOOD DEPICTIONS OF PARIS AS A WONDERLAND, THE REALITY WAS SOMEWHAT DIFFERENT"

123

guerilla attacks in Paris by the National Liberation Front, fighting for the independence of Algiers. During demonstrations to protest France's involvement in the situation in Egypt, one of the crew on *Love in the Afternoon* was reportedly hit by a missile and died later in hospital.

Audrey was given an armed bodyguard and was taken on detours to find a safe route to the studio, but with the painful childhood memories of war, she was keen to finish the production as quickly as possible, as was Billy Wilder. Once filming was complete, Audrey, as always, negotiated to keep her Givenchy wardrobe. She requested that the designer make each gown with adjustable seams as she liked to have the option of giving them as gifts to friends. After wearing the film's opera gown to an event in Los Angeles, she passed it on to her childhood friend, Tanja Star-Bussmann, to celebrate the birth of Tanja's daughter in 1958.

Love in the Afternoon would be Audrey's last movie of the fifties where she was able to request Givenchy for the costumes. She might have stipulated his services in her contract where possible, but when it came to her next films, the Givenchy wardrobe would not have worked for her characters: a nun in *The Nun's Story*, a forest sprite in *Green Mansions* and a ranch girl in *The Unforgiven.*

"I did not do the movie where she played a nun," Givenchy wryly reflected in 1989. "She wore something that looked like a bag." [53]

Audrey's life over the next few years involved extensive travel. *The Nun's Story* (1959) was filmed in Italy and the Congo, and such was the depth of feeling and commitment she brought to the part, she was rewarded with another Oscar nomination. "We worked strenuously on

"GIVENCHY WOULD LATER REMEMBER SOMETHING INCREDIBLY TOUCHING THAT SHE HAD SAID TO HIM, THAT 'WHEN I WEAR A WHITE BLOUSE OR LITTLE SUIT THAT YOU CREATE FOR ME, I HAVE THE FEELING OF BEING PROTECTED BY THAT BLOUSE OR SUIT – AND THIS PROTECTION IS VERY IMPORTANT TO ME.'"

AUDREY HEPBURN ON FRENCH DESIGNER GIVENCHY

location in the humid, intense heat of the Congo and freezing cold of Belgium," she said. "It made me realize as never before the effect of climate on one's system. It's very difficult to have energy or drive in the tropics." [54] She was glad to have some respite and went to Paris to visit Givenchy, where she was fitted for pieces for her personal wardrobe.

For both the London and Amsterdam premieres of *The Nun's Story*, Audrey wore the same Givenchy gown, created in his Paris salon, and which gave her the confidence to face all those crowds. Givenchy

During filming breaks in *Love in the Afternoon,*
Audrey would visit her husband, Mel Ferrer, at
Cap d'Antibes on the French Riviera.

Audrey attends Hubert de Givenchy's salon
for fittings of the gown worn to the London
premiere of *The Nun's Story* (1959).

would later remember something incredibly touching that she had said to him, that "When I wear a white blouse or little suit that you create for me, I have the feeling of being protected by that blouse or suit – and this protection is very important to me.'" [55]

Audrey continued to visit Paris to view his collections every season. When she selected items for her personal wardrobe, she would pay full price rather than expecting to be given them gratis. She was also generous when it came to sharing her love for Givenchy with friends. When British actress Deborah Kerr and screenwriter Peter Viertel married in 1960, Audrey's wedding present to her friend was a pink suit personally selected by her from his collection.

After completing *The Nun's Story*, Audrey travelled to Los Angeles, where she was directed by husband Mel in MGM's *Green Mansions* (1959), opposite Anthony Perkins. Audrey's character, a rainforest dwelling girl, Rima, with a fawn as her companion, falls in love with a Venezuelan explorer. While the film shared similarities with *Ondine*, it was received poorly on release in 1959. Audrey then travelled to Durango, Mexico, to make *The Unforgiven* (1960), a Western directed by John Huston and starring Burt Lancaster. While filming a horse-riding stunt, she was thrown from her horse and broke her back as a result of the awkward landing. She recovered in hospital and returned to complete the film in a back brace hidden under her costume, but having been pregnant at the time, she later miscarried.

Audrey wanted nothing more than to have a family of her own and after a series of devastating miscarriages, she gave birth to a son, Sean Hepburn Ferrer, in Lucerne, Switzerland, in 1960. Now that she was a mother, she was careful as to what movies she signed up to do. It was not just the script she considered, but also the location. She chose the ones that wouldn't take her too far from her home in Switzerland, and if the film was set in Paris, where she was close to Givenchy, then the answer was more likely to be yes.

CHAPTER SIX

Paris in the Summertime

AFTER THE BIRTH OF SEAN, AUDREY TOOK
A LONG BREAK FROM ACTING SO SHE COULD
ENJOY NEW MOTHERHOOD AT THE FAMILY
HOME IN PEACEFUL BÜRGENSTOCK, WHERE
THE ALPINE AIR WAS SOOTHING TO HER
SOUL. STILL, SHE CONTINUED TO TRAVEL
EXTENSIVELY FOR HER HUSBAND'S WORK.

They were in Paris while Mel made *L'homme à Femmes* (1960) with Catherine Deneuve, which was followed by trips to the Ivory Coast, LA and Rome. As she said, their life was "six months here, three months somewhere else, four months somewhere else, constantly renting houses and packing, shipping". [56]

During one visit to Paris in 1960, Audrey was photographed by the British photographer Cecil Beaton at his studios. "She has lost her elfin looks," said Beaton, "now she has a new womanly beauty." [57] This new Audrey would be apparent in her return to the screen; in a film that would become entwined with her persona, even if the character was quite different to the real Audrey.

After turning down high-calibre projects including *Cleopatra* and *West Side Story*, which went to Elizabeth Taylor and Natalie Wood respectively, she finally said yes to an adaptation of Truman Capote's novella *Breakfast at Tiffany's*. It told the story of a flighty yet incredibly chic New York escort, Holly Golightly, who refuses to be trapped by marriage. George Axelrod's screenplay disguised some of the forbidden aspects of Holly, such as her penchant for weed, the hints of bisexuality and the illegitimate child, and Paramount insisted that rather than a call girl, she was really a "kook", one of the hip words of the sixties. The film would sit on the boundaries between the conservatism of the previous decade and the permissiveness and youthful rebellion of the years that followed.

Blake Edwards' snappy directorial style, and the non-conformist attitude of Holly, proved a match for the European filmmakers, who were making a dent in culture and challenging Hollywood's dominance. Jean-Luc Godard's *À Bout de Souffle* (*Breathless*) had been released in 1960 and Jean Seberg, with her pixie cut and *New York Herald Tribune* T-shirt, represented the new generation of independent American women living in Paris. Holly Golightly was a New York-based incarnation of that freedom-loving woman, who similarly makes smoking an art form and has affairs with dangerous men. She lives in an apartment on her own, which was

William Holden and Audrey with the Eiffel
Tower in the background, 1962.

PREVIOUS Audrey wearing Givenchy on a
Bateau Mouche on the Seine, ahead of filming
Paris When it Sizzles in 1962.

OVERLEAF Givenchy's iconic little black dress
for Audrey's character Holly Golightly in
Breakfast at Tiffany's (1961).

133

almost unheard of for a woman in 1961, and she wears elegant black, which at that point was closely associated with femme fatales or French women.

In France, *Breakfast at Tiffany's* was called *Diamants sur Canapé*, meaning "Diamonds on Toast", which encapsulated its hip, quirky elegance. There was something very Parisian about the film, where Holly's catchphrase, "Quel beast!" was uttered everywhere following its release in cinemas, and with the sharp styling of both Audrey and her co-star, Patricia Neal (with her character '2E' Failenson in costumes by French-American designer Pauline Trigère) as if the French flavour allowed for some of the more risqué aspects. After all, what happened in France was more liberal. As film critic Barry Norman once said, Paris is depicted as "a place where something delicious and probably naughty is about to happen any minute. Actually, Paris isn't really like that at all."

Audrey was the good girl of cinema and Holly, who steps out of a cab at 5 a.m. in a Givenchy evening gown because she's not been to bed yet, was the archetype bad girl, who in fifties Hollywood would be punished, but here, she receives the happy ending. As Sam Wasson writes in *Fifth Avenue, 5 A.M.: Audrey Hepburn, Breakfast at Tiffany's, and the Dawn of the Modern Woman*: "people who encountered Audrey's Holly Golightly in 1961 experienced, for the very first time, a glamorous fantasy life of wild, kooky independence and sophisticated sexual freedom; best of all, it was a fantasy they could make real."

The role of Holly was a departure for Audrey; she'd never played such an iconoclastic woman before, and for all Holly's madcap antics, with her phone kept in the suitcase and the ginger cat she allows to roam free, she was the most openly permissive character of her career up until that point. Henry Mancini's "Moon River" and Audrey's raw singing voice as she strums a guitar on her fire escape, brought an emotional heart to the film. She had been reluctant to take on such a part, and given that Capote had wanted Marilyn Monroe to play

Holly, but was vetoed by producers, she was worried she wouldn't be able to bring this complicated figure to life.

Audrey was reunited with Hubert de Givenchy and his clothes once again gave her the security she needed, particularly with all the anxiety she felt in taking on the part. "I should be a stylish Holly Golightly, even if that's all I can contribute," she said ruefully to a reporter on set. While Edith Head created some of the supplementary costumes, Givenchy designed the two little black dresses for Holly, as stipulated in Truman Capote's original story, as well as a hot pink silk cocktail dress studded with gold appliqués. Capote's description of Holly Golightly in "a slim, cool black dress, black sandals, a pearl choker", "her chic thinness" and a "pair of dark glasses blotted out her eyes" conjured up the character brought to life on screen.

Costume fittings took place at Givenchy's new salon at 3 Avenue George V, a former hotel which he had moved into in 1959. His name

"HE'S MY GREAT LOVE, AND HE'S MARVELLOUS FOR ME."

AUDREY HEPBURN ON GIVENCHY

135

was emblazoned on the curved balcony on the building's facade and the interiors accentuated his classic elegance; the Art Nouveau wrought-iron railings clinging to the winding staircase and the white-painted rooms flooded with natural light from its vast windows.

Here, in his breezy, grand atelier, he created a sweeping black gown to transition from a dark nightclub to early-morning window shopping at Tiffany's and the shorter cocktail dress worn with a huge eye-concealing hat decorated with an over-sized ribbon. Riccardo Tisci, former creative director of Givenchy, described the long black dress as a perfect example of 1960s style, as it was chic at the front and sensual and Parisian at the back.

"Givenchy has designed lovely clothes for me in this picture," Audrey told *Cosmopolitan* magazine in February 1961. "He's my great love, and

Audrey as Gabrielle Simpson in *Paris When
it Sizzles* (1964), dressed in an Eau de Nil
Givenchy suit.

he's marvellous for me. I've been a good customer of his for many years. He made the first dresses I ever had from a good fashion house."

Audrey and Givenchy were incredibly close and this understanding translated into the designs he created for her. Olivier de Givenchy, nephew of Hubert, recalled a note that the designer received from Audrey in 1960. While flying from Paris to Los Angeles, after fittings for her character Holly Golightly, she had scribbled down on the back of an Air France envelope, in French and English, all the reasons she loved him. [58]

Shooting began in October 1960, with exteriors filmed in New York, including outside Tiffany's on Fifth Avenue, and then interiors on the Paramount lot in Hollywood. Once completed, she and Mel returned to Paris, while he made the French ensemble film *The Devil and the Ten Commandments* (1962). Audrey was back in Los Angeles to make the drama *The Children's Hour*, with Shirley MacLaine and James Garner, and at the end of December 1961, after attending the premieres in New York and Boston, she and her husband travelled to Rome, where it was said she was looking exhausted and suffering from an asthma flare-up in their cold rented villa.

Audrey still owed Paramount one more film as part of her contract, which was set to expire at the end of 1962. William Holden, her *Sabrina* co-star, was also in the same position, and with both stars wishing to film in Paris over the summer of 1962, a new Paris-set movie was tailor-made for them.

Paramount Studios commissioned George Axelrod, *Breakfast at Tiffany's* scriptwriter, to pen a script, which was lightly based on the 1952 French film *La Fête à Henriette* (*Holiday for Henrietta*) and starring Hildegard Knef. It was initially to be called *Together in Paris*, but a new title was borrowed from a line in Cole Porter's 1953 song "I Love Paris".

William Holden plays a successful Hollywood screenwriter, Richard Benson, who has only 48 hours to churn out a story to fulfill his generous contract. To avert disaster, his studio hires a young and imaginative assistant, Gabrielle Simpson, played by Audrey, to come to his luxury apartment in Paris to help him finish the script. Axelrod often skewered the film industry in his writings, as he was frequently frustrated and depressed by the censorship they typically placed on his sex comedies. So he designed it to be a parody of Hollywood and its stereotypes and movie genres, with overpaid and gin-soaked scriptwriters working on the hoof.

Gabrielle, who owes a resemblance to Jo in *Funny Face* in her quest to search out the avant-garde, is in admiration of the New Wave filmmakers. Their experimentalism is placed in contrast with Hollywood-types like Benson, who describes himself as "more of an old wave man myself", and the New Wave, like Existentialism in *Funny Face*, is parodied for being pretentious and trying too hard to be cool. Gabrielle, a free spirit, who says she has previously conducted a survey on the "depravity" of Paris, tells Benson she has arranged a date with an actor for Bastille Day, where they have planned out the perfect schedule.

"We're going to spend the whole day together. Starting with breakfast at this little cafe we go to. Then we're going to dance from one end of Paris to the other. The opera at five, then to the guards and the singing of 'Marseillaise', and off to Montmartre for the fireworks. And then supper and champagne, and, you know, live."

This inspires Benson to come up with a concept about a simple Parisian girl, who looks just like Gabrielle, and her perfect Bastille Day. As Gabrielle helps Richard Benson complete the script for a film called *The Girl Who Stole the Eiffel Tower*, they imagine it as a spy drama, a Western and a musical. The movie veers between the apartment setting and the fantasy sequences around Paris, as it darts between different drafts of the scripts, and with knowing cameos from Tony Curtis, Mel Ferrer and the voice of Frank Sinatra. The finished piece may have been a confusing mish-mash of concepts, but at least it had a pretty Parisian setting.

Audrey arrived at Paris's Orly Airport at the start of July 1962 in the company of the actor Anthony Perkins, who was visiting the city to attend an awards ceremony. Rather than checking into the Hotel

Audrey with William Holden during the filming
of *Paris When it Sizzles*, at La Grande Cascade
restaurant in the Bois de Boulogne, Paris.

Raphaël, she and Mel rented Château Crespières, an old Bourbon château on the road to Fontainebleau. It was a sprawling mansion with huge gardens, which would allow her some space and privacy, where she could enjoy time with her son and with Mel, in between his other filming commitments. William Holden flew into Paris from Switzerland, where he'd been skiing, and the red carpet was rolled out for him at the George V hotel – "The film is an unabashed comedy. I've been waiting a long time for a fun part," he told reporters. [59]

As well as renting its rooms to some of the cast and crew, the Art Deco George V hotel, built in 1928, was also a location in the film, as its terrace with views to the Eiffel Tower was used as part of Benson's penthouse apartment, set on the Champs-Élysées. To celebrate the start of the production, a cocktail party was held for the cast, writer and director on a Bateau Mouche on the Seine, where they enjoyed the views of the cityscape as they cruised past the Eiffel Tower, Notre-Dame and under its gilded bridges. Photographer Roger Viollet, alongside invited media, snapped images from this press event, with Audrey in Givenchy – a navy and white silk cocktail dress, and her hair in the loose beehive style of Holly Golightly.

The cocktail event was a taster of what the film aimed to be – a love letter to the city – but depicting it as hip, fashionable and swinging. The city's cafés and parks were used for the exterior locations and as Paramount said in its publicity, "a pot-pourri of gay and bizarre Parisian backgrounds with the city assuming the role of a sort of 'third star' of the production."

Director Richard Quine and his co-producer George Axelrod flew over Paris in a helicopter, charting some of the locations they thought could be interesting. These included the forest glade of Les Yvelines, the Place Dauphine, the point of the Île de la Cité where they said fisherman and students mixed together, the Bois de Boulogne near to the waterfall and its smart outdoor restaurant, and the facade of the Quai du Voltaire hostelry, where Baudelaire, Richard Wagner and Oscar Wilde once lived. In the opening sequence, filmed at the Hotel

141

Audrey arriving with the actor Anthony
Perkins at Orly Airport, Paris, in July 1962.

PARIS IN THE SUMMERTIME

du Cap-Eden-Roc, Antibes, Noël Coward plays a movie producer doing business in the company of a bevy of bikini-clad women.

The film then cuts to a shot of the Eiffel Tower – the instantly recognizable symbol of Paris – and Benson baking on his penthouse terrace. We first see Gabrielle in her Eau de Nil Givenchy suit on her way to begin her assignment at Benson's Champs-Élysées apartment. She passes by the puppet show at Guignol des Champs-Élysées, a comment on the theatricality of Paris, and on her role in helping manipulate characters to create a movie. Benson's terrace has a perfect view of the Eiffel Tower, which he describes as "that rather grotesque object looming so prominently on the horizon ... I had it moved there to remind me of what town I'm in." As he begins writing the script, he can't decide which iconic Parisian landmark to begin with – the Eiffel Tower, Sacré-Coeur or the Grand Palais – but he wants to give the audience "the taste and smell of the real Paris" so he inexplicably chooses the exterior of Christian Dior, with Marlene Dietrich stepping out of a white Bentley. He quickly scrunches up that page.

For Audrey, the major benefit of Paris was being close to Hubert de Givenchy again. He came to her home in Switzerland two months before the start of the production to do the initial designs and fittings, and they discussed the requirements for the character. Givenchy didn't just create the clothes for Audrey that he thought attractive, he carefully read the script and discussed concepts, to design costumes that worked with the narrative. The wardrobe was expected to bridge reality with fantasy, for a typist and her alter ego as the star of the invented movie. The action took place over Bastille Day, in the height of summer, so the wardrobe had to fit with the balmy, and sometimes stifling, heat. The costumes were then created in his Paris workrooms, which included the Eau de Nil wool suit, a clementine cocktail dress,

143

Taking a ride past Notre-Dame Cathedral on a Bateau Mouche on the Seine, with William Holden in 1962.

an ivory linen dress with a blue belt and a blue peignoir for one of the imagined sequences.

Audrey's press representative Nadia Marculescu told reporters: "Audrey, of course, gets her personal wardrobe from Givenchy so it is so much easier to come up with a film wardrobe since the designer knows just what's best for her. Often there's little difference between her wardrobe on screen and in her private life. Givenchy had to make the clothes rather simple in keeping with the wardrobe that an American secretary might wear in Paris. Naturally, one of Givenchy's little suits is perfect for the secretary." [60]

The majority of the interiors were shot at Studios de Boulogne in Paris, where Audrey had previously made *Love in the Afternoon*. The studio's permanent crew remembered her well from her time during the making of that film. Wardrobe woman Marguerite Brachet recalled: "Madame Hepburn was a delightful child, then, and is one now." [61] Here, she requested dressing room number 55, which she believed was lucky, as it was the same number as her Paramount dressing room for *Breakfast at Tiffany's* and the one she was assigned in *Roman Holiday*.

The film's director, Richard Quine, was engaged to the actress Kim Novak, who he had been tasked with guiding to stardom when she was first signed to Columbia Pictures in the early fifties. She arrived in Paris to visit Quine on set and according to her spokesperson, "Miss Novak loves Paris and is having a fine time. She brought her fall clothes and plans to stay for a month or so." [62]

Filming got off to a difficult start when Audrey complained after seeing the daily rushes by cinematographer Claude Renoir, nephew of Jean Renoir, who perhaps favoured a more realistic vision rather than the flattering light diffusions of Hollywood. She asked that he be replaced by Charles B. Lang Jr, who had lit and filmed her so beautifully in *Sabrina*. Richard Quine agreed to do as his star insisted, but it was a decision that would cause problems with his French crew: "Of course, firing a Renoir is tantamount to

The roof terrace of the George V Hotel, the set of *Paris When it Sizzles*, with director Richard Quine and co-star William Holden.

treason in France, so the unions raised hell and threatened to go out on strike," he said. [63]

A reporter from the *Philadelphia Inquirer* visited the set to watch Audrey and William Holden at work. She observed Holden acting out a scene in what she described as one of the most luxurious sets she'd seen in Paris. The production crew had constructed an expensive-looking penthouse apartment, "the type of place an American would insist on renting". She also described Audrey as "nervously darting in and out of her dressing room waiting for her next scene. In it, she would wear a blue organza peignoir embroidered in white and ruffled down the front. It was hanging there awaiting word from the set that everything was in readiness for the star. Audrey's stand-in, dressed in a sleazy version of the Givenchy peignoir, would go through the grueling preliminary steps of setting up lights." [64]

Rather than sizzling in summer, the weather in Paris was often drizzling, which caused issues for the production in being able to stick with the schedule. The crew would phone the Le Bureau de Météorologie every night at 6 p.m. to check on the weather forecast, which was measured by the sky-casters at the top of the Eiffel Tower and the highest point of Montmartre. If the forecast for the next day was promising, they moved the six tons of equipment to the location site and notified their 300 extras that they would be required for one of the outdoor scenes set at La Grande Cascade restaurant in the Bois de Boulogne. [65]

Audrey found the shoot exhausting. She woke at 4 a.m. every morning to be ready to be picked up by limousine, which drove her from the château to the studios, a journey that could take an hour. After a long day's filming, making frustratingly slow progress, she wouldn't be home until eight in the evening. Gossip columnist Dorothy Kilgallen speculated that Audrey was considering moving into some "groovy Left Bank hotel" because she felt she was "missing too much of the Gay Paree fun", but in reality, if she was considering going back to Hotel Raphaël, it was to make the commute to the studios much easier.

She arrived on set every day typically wearing the same outfit: a classic shirt tied at the waist, with a pair of red slacks. She would then change into her Givenchy costumes, which were the usual understated elegance, but in bright colours to reflect the sunniness of the script – "Everything he makes is just right for me," she told a reporter. [66]

She described how she preferred neutrals in her own wardrobe due to her own nomadic existence: "I like conservative colors such as beige or black, which will look right at almost any hour of the day or evening and in almost any weather. This enables me, too, to cut down on accessories. I have only black or beige shoes and bags and wear only white three-quarter length gloves. The only exceptions are an

"EVERYTHING HE MAKES IS JUST RIGHT FOR ME"

AUDREY HEPBURN ON GIVENCHY

evening purse and one pair of white satin shoes." [67]

While Audrey was at first happy to be reunited with her *Sabrina* co-star, who she'd had a love affair with at the time, William Holden was struggling with alcoholism, further exacerbated by the character he was playing: a writer who needs a Bloody Mary to function. During filming, he was dating French model and *The Pink Panther* actress Capucine, a close friend of Hepburn's. But his drinking led him to make awkward declarations to Audrey that he was still in love with her, as he had been during the making of *Sabrina*. He would get so inebriated during the day that he would have to be carried to his car. A snippet in the gossip columns revealed that he was seen at Paris's bistros as late as 5 a.m. and that clearly, he was deeply troubled by something.

One evening, after a day of drinking, Holden climbed up the tree that led to Audrey's dressing room, with a drunken idea of playing Romeo to her Juliet, but he slipped and fell. He was sent to a clinic at Château de

Audrey and husband Mel snapped by
paparazzo Pierluigi Praturlon in Paris, 1962.

Garches to get sober and in the meantime, with Paramount threatening to shut down production due to rising costs, Tony Curtis, at the peak of his career with recent hits *Some Like it Hot* (1959) and *Spartacus* (1960) was hired to step in. He was flown into Paris, put up at the George V hotel and written into a fantasy sequence where he played Audrey's imaginary love interest. As Curtis remembered in his memoirs: "Axelrod and Quine frantically wrote a couple of new scenes and I worked with Audrey. I did about five or six days and then finally Holden came back to work. They just needed to fill that time."[68]

The official version of events was a different story. It was claimed that Holden was absent due to minor eye surgery, that Curtis's involvement was due to the filmmakers' dissatisfaction with the French actors who had auditioned to play Audrey's boyfriend and that Curtis had volunteered for the part while he was on holiday in Paris.

It was this confusion of ideas, as if it was being made up on the spot, which left the studio with concerns around its quality and so the release was put on hold until 1964, after Audrey's next film, *Charade* (1963), had come out to glowing reviews. As her biographer, Alexander Walker, wrote, "*Paris When It Sizzles* was a soufflé which refused to rise." The *Hollywood Reporter* praised Charles Lang's Technicolor photography, which gave "fresh beauty to the beautiful city", but the reviews were generally unfavourable. Audrey, and the consistency in her comic performance, remained unscathed. She would always be fond of Holden, but he slipped further into alcoholism, and in Italy in 1966, his drink-driving resulted in the death of another driver. While he continued to have some success in his career with *The Wild Bunch* (1969) and *Network* (1976), he died in 1981, after hitting his head when drunk.

The credits featured a surprising, and a little absurd, mention for Hubert de Givenchy. As well as his wardrobe, he also earned a credit for Audrey's scent. Givenchy had created a perfume, L'Interdit, especially for her, with its name referring to its exclusivity; that it was only for women who possessed her elegance or beauty.

CHAPTER SEVEN

Ice Cream on the River Seine

JUST AS PRODUCTION WAS WINDING UP ON *PARIS WHEN IT SIZZLES*, AUDREY WAS OFFERED ANOTHER SCRIPT FOR A MOVIE THAT WAS TO BE FILMED IN PARIS, AND WHERE ITS FAMOUS LANDMARKS WERE TO PLAY AN IMPORTANT PART OF THE STORY.

It was a thriller with Cary Grant, to be directed by Stanley Donen, with whom she had previously worked on *Funny Face*, and, almost immediately, she said yes.

Donen had recently directed Cary Grant in the romantic comedy *Indiscreet* (1958), with Ingrid Bergman, and he was keen to team him with Audrey. To add a further tempting morsel, he opted to make the film in Paris, as he knew Audrey preferred to be close to her son Sean and husband Mel, whose work commitments kept him in Europe.

To carry her through the shooting schedule, she extended the lease on the château near Fontainebleau for another four months and spoke with Hubert de Givenchy to begin preparations for his next assignment. She completed a long night shoot for *Paris When It Sizzles* and the next day went for wardrobe consultations at the Givenchy salon for the 19 pieces required for *Charade*.

"It was one of those quick and effective deals when everything seems to fall into place," said her agent, Henry Rogers. "Audrey had known Cary Grant for years and they fit each other to a tee, both sporting the same air of vivacious mischief, yet they had never worked together as a team." [69]

The script was by Peter Stone, an American writer who had lived in Paris for 10 years, and who used his knowledge of the city to inform the film's settings. As James Coburn, who played one of the criminals, told Audrey's biographer Barry Paris: "Peter Stone knew Paris very well because he'd lived there as a writer on the Île de France, right by Notre-Dame. Did you know that he wrote it specifically for Cary Grant and Audrey Hepburn?"

Stone chose the title because his story was constructed from three separate elements, of suspense, romance and comedy – like the three different scenes in acting out a game of charades – and because of this, it was described as "the Hitchcock thriller that Hitchcock never made". It was a mix of romantic comedy and *North by Northwest* adventure, with post-modern humour, a jazzy, psychedelic title sequence and with the city as a backdrop to the thrills.

Cary Grant and Audrey Hepburn in the
Jardins des Champs-Élysées during the
filming of *Charade*.

PREVIOUS The banks of the Seine were a
prominent filming location for *Charade* (1964).

Audrey plays Reggie Lampert, who discovers her husband has been murdered for his hidden treasures, and now she is under threat from the same criminal gang. Cary Grant is the American Treasury agent who has been assigned to recover these valuables, and who operates under a number of assumed names, beginning with Peter Joshua.

Despite being two of the biggest stars in Hollywood, Cary Grant and Audrey Hepburn had only met on a couple of occasions and so Stanley Donen arranged for them to have a proper sit-down together at an Italian restaurant in Paris. Audrey was nervous about meeting Grant, and as she and Donen waited for him at the table, she told her director how tense she was. She could hardly believe she was going to make a film with him: "I'm sure I'll never get through dinner, much less the picture," she confessed.

Cary sailed into the restaurant, looking debonair in a tan suit, and Audrey, as humble as always, stood up to shake his hand. He could tell she was nervous and so as they took their seats, he tried to teach her some of the relaxation techniques he'd been learning as part of his interest in alternative wellness. "Sit down," he told Audrey, "put your hands on the table. Rest your forehead on your hands. Now take a deep breath and relax."

As she followed his instructions, Audrey's elbow knocked over the full bottle of red wine on the table and it spilled onto Grant's tan suit. She was mortified ("like a child who'd disgraced herself at a party," according to Donen) as people at other tables turned to look at the spectacle. Grant coolly stripped off his jacket, handed it to the maître d', who whisked it away to their dry cleaner, and continued with dinner in his shirt, all the while reassuring Audrey not to worry. [70]

Grant just "nonchalantly removed his jacket," said Audrey, "and pretended, very convincingly, that the stain would simply go away... I felt terrible and kept apologizing, but Cary was so dear about it. The next day he sent me a box of caviar with a little note telling me not to feel bad." [71]

The incident inspired Stanley Donen to include a humorous reference to it in the film. As Audrey and Grant stroll along the Seine, near to the Pont de l'Archevêché, with Notre-Dame looming in the background, they stop at an ice-cream cart. He buys her a chocolate glacé and she accidentally swipes his expensive suit with her cone. "Working with Cary is so easy," Audrey said. "He does all the acting – you just react. It's that simple."

As with the majority of her co-stars up to this point, Grant was much older than Audrey. He was 59 during filming, compared to her 34, and in keeping with Peter Stone's wry script, the age difference is played up to.

"Here it comes, the fatherly talk," Reggie says. "You forget I'm already a widow."

"So was Juliet, at 15," Peter shoots back.

"I'm not 15."

"Well, that's your trouble. You're too old for me."

But the age difference didn't seem as pronounced as her pairings with Fred Astaire or Gary Cooper because Reggie is, at the beginning of the film, a married woman considering a divorce and then a widow.

"AUDREY WAS ONCE AGAIN BACK AT THE STUDIOS DE BOULOGNE, A PLACE WHERE SHE FELT AT EASE"

"I admit I came to Paris to escape American Provincial, but that doesn't mean I'm ready for French Traditional," she tells her friend Sylvie, who suggests she follow the Parisian method, by staying married to her rich husband, but indulging in extra-marital affairs.

Audrey was once again back at the Studios de Boulogne, a place where she felt at ease, given that she had formed a bond with the same crew from both *Love in the Afternoon* and *Paris When It Sizzles*.

"You may call me a permanent fixture at the Studios de Boulogne," she said at the time. "I am one of those who can say I remember

when..." The same furniture from *Love in the Afternoon* was being recycled for the set dressing in *Charade*, which added a degree of poignancy, given that Gary Cooper had passed away the year before, at the age of sixty, after being diagnosed with an aggressive form of prostate cancer. "I don't like to think of it. It's sad. We loved him so," she added. [72]

As was her routine when filming *Paris When It Sizzles*, she made her way to the studios from the château by chauffeur-driven car every morning, or to the outdoor shoots at various locations around Paris. Mel was beginning work on the big budget production of *The Fall of the Roman Empire* (1964), to be shot in Rome and Madrid, and when he was away, the large château must have felt lonely. Audrey checked into the Raphaël for some of the time, which was more convenient for the night shoots around the city. When Mel returned to Paris, he stayed in the château on his own, leading to rumours of a separation. Their marriage had long been under scrutiny, with a common belief that Mel was dominant and controlling, while Audrey was too nice to stand up for herself. She'd answered these criticisms head-on in an article for *Photoplay* in April 1956, entitled 'My Husband Doesn't Run Me'.

Cary Grant was staying at his ex-wife Barbara Hutton's Paris apartment during filming and he and Audrey would often socialize over dinner and drinks. Over the festive season the Ferrers held a New Year's Eve party in their château for Stanley Donen and his third wife, Adelle, Peter Stone and his wife, Mary, and Cary Grant and his 25-year-old girlfriend, actress Dyan Cannon. It was a lavish affair, befitting the grand location, with servants in white gloves serving huge baked potatoes with ladles of sour cream and Russian caviar.

The opening sequence of *Charade* was filmed at Les Chalets du Mont d'Arbois in Megève, Switzerland, the playground of the rich ski set, which sits in the shadow of Mont Blanc. Audrey's character, Reggie, is dressed in a chic hooded ski outfit, designed by Givenchy, and when she encounters Grant's Peter Joshua, immediately we see a woman who knows her own mind and who has a wry sense of

Givenchy designed a hooded ski outfit for the opening
scenes of *Charade*, at Les Chalets du Mont d'Arbois,
Megève, in the French Alps.

PREVIOUS Audrey chooses an ice cream on the banks
of the Seine, while filming a scene in *Charade*.

humour: "I already know an awful lot of people and until one of them dies, I couldn't possibly meet anyone else," she informs him.

When Reggie arrives back at her grand apartment in Paris, dressed in a latte-coloured wool coat and hat, she discovers that her husband has stripped its baroque, high-ceilinged rooms of furnishings and that he has been murdered and thrown off the Paris to Bordeaux train. Peter Joshua arrives at the apartment, the exterior of which was located at 7 Avenue Velasquez, on the other side of Parc Monceau from Givenchy's original salon, and takes her to the Hôtel Saint-Jacques on the rue des Écoles, in the Latin Quarter.

"WOULDN'T IT BE NICE IF WE COULD BE LIKE HIM? GENE KELLY. REMEMBER WHEN HE DANCED DOWN HERE BY THE RIVER WITHOUT A CARE IN THE WORLD IN AN AMERICAN IN PARIS"

AUDREY HEPBURN IN *CHARADE*

From there, they visit Parisian landmarks including the US Embassy and the famed produce market at Les Halles, a glass and iron structure dating from the 1850s, which was controversially flattened to make way for new building developments (including the Pompidou Centre) in the seventies. The Carré Marigny (Marigny Square) is where Hepburn and Grant watch the children's puppet show at Théâtre Vrai Guignolet and where they explore the postage stamp market, which had been located there since the nineteenth century.

Like Audrey, cinematographer Charles Lang had gone straight from working on *Paris When It Sizzles* to *Charade*, and in interview with *American Cinematographer* magazine, he said this proved to be an advantage: "It was actually quite a break, in that I continued to work with one of the same stars, Audrey Hepburn, and with substantially

Cary Grant and Audrey with Notre-Dame in the background, during the filming of *Charade*.

the same French production crew I had on the other picture. They were used to me and I to them, and we got along fine – even though I never learned French much more than to say a few words and talk with my hands. But they were a fine bunch and we worked very well together." [73]

While much of *Paris When It Sizzles'* interiors were shot in the studio, Stanley Donen wanted to take advantage of the rich Technicolor to bring Paris's real locations to life and so Charles Lang used his lighting skills to work within the confines of places like Les Halles and the St Varennes Metro station, and at the resort at Megève. Twelve truckloads of equipment were brought by road from Paris to the Alps, including interior sets in case the weather turned. The terrace sequences were shot on location at the resort and one of the challenges for Lang was the sequence by the indoor swimming pool, where the lights picked up reflection on the glass enclosure.

"While we were up there, we had a blizzard that lasted for several days so we built an interior 'cover' set," said Lang. "The set represented the nightclub lounge where Audrey Hepburn runs downstairs to make a phone call and carries on a lengthy scene in the phone booth. The company built that little room with the phone booth in a vacant garage – and believe me, it was mighty cold working there." [74]

Charade was another cinematic love letter to the city, with knowing references to cultural moments that had taken place there before. As they walk along the Seine, Reggie Lampert (Audrey) observes, "Wouldn't it be nice if we could be like him? Gene Kelly. Remember when he danced down here by the river without a care in the world in *An American in Paris*?"

They glance up at Notre-Dame cathedral and Cary Grant's character jokes: "Oh, who put that there?"

They have dinner on a Bateau Mouche at night-time, sailing past the silhouettes of the city's buildings, and the glow of street lights on its bridges. At one point in the cruise, the boat shines its spotlight on couples embracing on the edge of the Seine, again reinforcing the idea of Paris as a city for lovers.

163 {

Audrey and Cary Grant in *Charade*,
enjoying a romantic evening cruise
on the Seine.

Audrey and Cary Grant take a break
during the making of *Charade*.

Much of the location shooting took place outdoors, and at night to avoid the crowds that would inevitably gather to gawk at two of the biggest movie stars in the world. This included the dramatic finale on the real subway cars in the Paris underground and in the colonnade of the Palais Royale, where its neo-classical columns act as a cover. During the night-shoot, the cast rested between takes at a local bistro, where Audrey used the telephone to check in with Mel.

With the winter of 1962 being one of the coldest on record, cast and crew struggled in the icy conditions. To help keep Audrey warm while filming outdoors, Givenchy designed a variety of thick wool coats with funnel necks paired with chi chi hats. "Wearing Givenchy's lovely simple clothes, wearing a jazzy little red coat and whatever little hat was then the fashion – I felt super," she later recalled.[75]

"You don't know how cold it was in Paris last winter," said Adelle Donen, wife of the director, in an interview to mark the film's release. "Everybody had on about three coats, except Audrey and Cary. Cary was stuck with a cotton raincoat. That scene with the Bateau Mouche going down the Seine – it looked gloriously romantic. There were ice blocks all around the boat and we had to have a machine to keep the whole thing from freezing completely." [76]

In one scene, Audrey wore a red funnel-neck coat teamed with a striking leopard-print hat, the epitome of 1960s European cool, and for the chase sequence in the Métro, she is dressed in yellow; making her more visible as she tries to hide from her pursuer.

Audrey ensured she kept all of the costumes after filming was completed and she would wear them over and over, or give them to friends. She was an early proponent of sustainability, and having survived hardship as a child, she retained the wartime mentality of frugality – "I don't replace clothes until they can't be worn. I'll wear the skirt of an old suit with sweaters. I had a red coat – the one in *Charade* – by Hubert, of course. I wore it until the threads began to separate and it was all shiny on the edges." [77]As for the navy-blue suit, worn with a white hat, she also kept it for future use, as she said, "I

just wore it for an instant. Most clothes that you wear in a film get so burned out by the lights, the material looks tired – and you become bored with them, you wear them so much." [78]

With its glamour, excitement, humour and suspense, *Charade* was lapped up by critics and audiences, with Pauline Kael in *The New Yorker* calling it "probably the best American film" of the year. As *Newsday* wrote in their review: "There are exotic locales – a skiing lodge in the French Alps, the midnight cruise down the Seine, the pre-dawn visit to Les Halles, a suspenseful ride in the Métro... producer-director Stanley Donen has even enlisted the typical Hitchcock heroine, the pale, slender refugee from the pages of *Vogue*."

Paris When It Sizzles and *Charade* had been made back-to-back, and as soon as Audrey completed work with Cary Grant, she had another project she was very much looking forward to. She had been informed by her agent during the making of *Charade* that the coveted role of Eliza Doolittle in *My Fair Lady* was hers. She was to be paid $1 million and it was the most ambitious film project ever undertaken by Warner Bros. She and her family lived in Los Angeles for the duration of filming and, afterwards, she embarked on a worldwide publicity tour. She returned to Paris for its lavish premiere at the Empire cinema in December 1964, dressed in Givenchy, with her hair styled at Alexandre de Paris and accompanied by husband Mel. During a press conference before the premiere, Audrey sweetly acted as French translator between the reporters and her co-star, Rex Harrison.

While her Edwardian costumes were designed by Cecil Beaton, the film offered a further collaboration between Audrey and Hubert de Givenchy. The Parisian designer reimagined her screen costumes with his own twist and Audrey then modelled these outfits for American *Vogue* in 1964, with photographs taken by Beaton.

The interior of the Varennes Métro station on Boulevard des Invalides, Paris, stood in for the Saint Jacques station in *Charade* (1963).

Despite her joy at playing Eliza, it came with some controversy. Julie Andrews, who had made the character her own on Broadway, had been passed over for the film adaptation in favour of Audrey, much to Andrews' disappointment. It was then revealed that Audrey's singing voice had been dubbed by the American soprano Marni Nixon, making it appear as if she took the coveted role without possessing the full credentials. Audrey did not earn the expected Oscar nomination and, that year, Andrews took home the award for *Mary Poppins*. Audrey received the first negative headlines of her career and she was without the usual protection of her press agent Henry Rogers, after parting company because of a row over her relationship with Givenchy. Audrey had always paid full price for her Givenchy couture and had agreed to be the face of his perfume, L'Interdit, without recompense. Mel felt she should at least receive a discount on clothes, or some bottles of perfume, but she didn't feel right about being paid as the designer was one of her closest friends. She was horrified that on her husband's behest, Rogers had approached Givenchy's brother, who handled finances, for compensation and in these circumstances, she felt she had no choice but to let her agent go. The situation put further strain on her marriage, which had been rocky for a while.

With a fresh start in mind, in 1965 she and Mel bought a farmhouse in Tolochenaz, in the hills above Lake Geneva, which they named La Paisable, or "the peaceful place". After the exhaustive shoot and publicity campaign around *My Fair Lady*, here was a chance to catch her breath. Before too long, she would be back in Paris to make another movie set in the City of Light, but this time, rather than a Cinderella story or a period piece, it would be representative of a new Audrey in synergy with the Swinging Sixties.

Audrey at the premiere of *My Fair Lady* at the Empire cinema, Paris, in December 1964.

CHAPTER EIGHT

The Swinging Sixties

WHEN AUDREY SPED PAST NOTRE-DAME
CATHEDRAL IN AN OPEN-TOP RED SPORTS
CAR, A VISION IN GLEAMING WHITE, FROM HER
HELMET HAT TO HER BUG-EYE SUNGLASSES
AND JACKET, IT FELT LIKE THE LAUNCH OF A
NEW, CULTURALLY HIP WOMAN.

The film was *How to Steal a Million*, and when released in 1966, it embodied sixties modernity, particularly with its playful "How to" title, the groovy Henry Mancini soundtrack and its self-referential jokes. ("Well for one thing, it gives Givenchy the night off," Peter O'Toole's character Simon Dermott tells Audrey [Nicole Bonnet], when he persuades her to disguise herself as a cleaner.)

Along with Jacqueline Kennedy, Audrey was continually at the top of the Best Dressed lists and as she had been the icon of the fifties, she moved seamlessly into what became known as "Mod" – a youth-led fashion of angular, clean lines and European pizzazz. Her figure was designed for this look, which celebrated slenderness over curves with its mini-skirts and neat-as-a-pin tailoring. Mod style was Mary Quant and London's King Road, bright colours and geometric op-art inspired prints, and by 1964, Parisian designers like Pierre Cardin, Paco Rabanne and André Courrèges were creating further Mod innovations. Audrey's off-white costume in the opening scenes of *How to Steal a Million* was reflective of the current fascination with all things Space Age. Courrèges in 1964 had launched his "Moon Girl" collection, using brilliant white and silver, with contrasting orange and red, and featuring helmet-style hats and thick plastic-rimmed sunglasses.

Hubert de Givenchy once again created the costumes for Audrey in *How to Steal a Million* and while they still followed his rule of elegant simplicity, they had an edge to them, suiting the pervasive youth culture movements at the time. The script, by Harry Kurnitz, was a comedy caper set in the fine art world, with scenes taking place in Paris's most famous luxury hotel, the Ritz, and in the city's rarefied restaurants and art galleries. It told the story of a fine art forger Charles Bonnet (Hugh Griffith), whose daughter, Nicole (played by Audrey), is worried he'll finally be caught when his supposed Cellini statue goes on display in one of Paris's most prestigious art galleries. To save him from being arrested, she hires a gentleman thief, Simon Dermott (Peter O'Toole) to help her steal the fake Cellini statue before it's revealed as a fraud.

Givenchy gave Audrey a hip Mod look for *How to Steal a Million* with a white helmet and sunglasses.

PREVIOUS Audrey during the filming of *How to Steal a Million* (1966) in a raspberry Givenchy coat.

Despite her reluctance to be too far from her home in Switzerland, Audrey always had a soft spot for Paris and she was pleased to be back at the Studios de Boulogne to begin filming in July 1965. This time she stayed in Paris while Mel was at home in Switzerland with their son, Sean. It only served to add to the speculation that their marriage was on the rocks.

The film, with its working title *How to Steal a Million Dollars and Live Happily Ever After*, was a reunion with William Wyler, the director who had guided a novice to Oscar-winning success in *Roman Holiday*, and Charles Lang as cinematographer. The sets were designed by Hungarian production designer Alexandre Trauner, who recreated the bar at the Ritz, the interior of Maxim's restaurant, and a fictitious art gallery. He also hired skilled imitators to recreate the forged Renoirs, van Goghs and Picassos required for the movie.

Givenchy was tasked with designing 24 costumes for the film, working to a generous $30,000 budget. Audrey wore shorter skirts than ever before, with out-there hats, modish checked jackets, caps and cord blazers and a stunning black lace dress with matching Venetian mask. William Wyler tested the costumes on colour film to see if they would photograph well and a number of changes were then made.

To further enhance her Mod make-over, Audrey was given a short, geometric hairstyle by Alexandre de Paris, the celebrity hairstylist to the stars who had created Elizabeth Taylor's trendsetting hair in *Cleopatra* (1963). His salon was located on the rue de Faubourg Saint-Honoré, in the heart of Paris's fashion district and featured a logo designed by his friend, the multi-talented artist Jean Cocteau. A further Cleopatra touch was the new look make-up by Alberto de Rossi, who used a heavy application of kohl and layered lashes upon lashes for bold, dark eyes. As was typical for an Audrey Hepburn picture, the fashion was paramount

Audrey at the Studios de Boulogne, during the
making of *How to Steal a Million*. Portrait by
Douglas Kirkland.

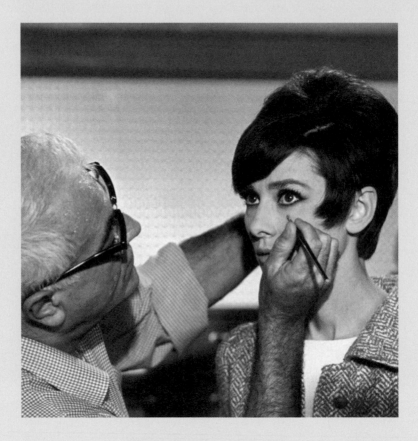

Make-up artist Alberto de Rossi
created a new look for Audrey in
How to Steal a Million.

and as she told a reporter on the set, "I always dreamt of the day when I would have enough closets – big ones. Some people dream of having a big swimming pool – with me, its closets." [79]

When we first see Nicole Bonnet in her cherry-red sports car, she's effortlessly cool, a little reckless, and she clearly enjoys her freedom. On hearing that her father has sold one of his forged paintings for a huge amount, she whizzes back to the family mansion, climbs out the car and up the sweeping steps, giving the audience a full look at her outfit – the white skirt, tights and shoes.

Nicole is reading an Alfred Hitchcock mystery magazine when she hears someone breaking into her home. She catches a thief, Simon Dermott (O'Toole), apparently in the process of stealing one of her father's paintings, and when the antique gun she's holding goes off accidentally, they both faint at the sight of his flesh wound. "I'm a society burglar," he claims. "I don't expect people to rush about shooting me."

"AS WAS TYPICAL FOR AN AUDREY HEPBURN PICTURE, THE FASHION WAS PARAMOUNT"

177

Dermott asks for a lift home and when he tells her he's staying at the Ritz, she replies, "You're a very chic burglar, aren't you?" She slings a raspberry wool coat over her nightgown and a pair of boots, and after climbing into his sports car, they race across the city at night. The camera follows above as she speeds around a fountain and they then pull into the Place Vendôme entrance to the Ritz. It was Audrey's return to the iconic hotel after its prominent appearance in *Love in the Afternoon* and not only was it now captured in colour, she was no longer the ingénue.

In one scene, Audrey wears one of her most sensual screen costumes, a black lace gown with a matching lace mask, which would remain one of her favourites: "I was trying to be mysterious and the mask was such a pretty way to be incognito. Hubert always had a wonderful understanding of the scenes," she would later say. [80]

Nicole has arranged to meet Simon in the bar at the Ritz, but wishes to disguise herself while asking him to mastermind a heist. He agrees to steal the fake Cellini, because he's clearly attracted to her and wants to use it as an excuse for a long, cosy lunch together:

"Look, it's early, why don't I show you the real Paris?" he says.

"That's very kind of you, but I live here. I was born in Paris."

"Oh, I forgot. Well, why don't you show me the real Paris?"

In another scene, they have dinner in the celebrity favourite restaurant, Maxim's, with the plush red and gold interior recreated on the studio lot, and which contrasts with Nicole's apple-green Givenchy suit. Other locations included the courtyard of the Musée Carnavalet, a museum dedicated to Paris history on 23 rue de Sévigné, which stood in for the exterior of the fictional Kleber-Lafayette Museum, where the heist takes place. The museum gate was filmed at rue des Francs-Bourgeois, in the Marais district, and a house in Neuilly-sur-Seine, on the junction of rue Parmentier and Boulevard Bineau, was the exterior of the Bonnet family home.

For one of the first times in her career, Audrey was paired with a younger male co-star, the devilishly handsome Peter O'Toole, who was three years younger, and the chemistry between them was evident. The two bonded during filming, particularly over the course of the 11 days it took to shoot the museum broom cupboard scenes, when Simon and Nicole realize the lust and love they feel for one another.

According to Audrey's biographers, O'Toole gave her the nickname "the Duke of Buckingham", due to her reaction to brandy while filming outside in the bitter cold. The nickname referred to a performance of *Richard III* by the nineteenth-century actor Edmund Kean, who got drunk with one of his cast mates before he was about to go on stage. Kean was noticeably slurring his speech and when heckled by an audience member, fired back, "If you think I'm drunk, wait until you see the Duke of Buckingham."

In this particular scene, Audrey was expected to walk across the street, climb into her car and drive off, but seeing that she was

179

The lace mask and dress designed by
Givenchy for *How to Steal a Million* was one of
Audrey's favourite movie costumes.

shivering from the cold, the hard-drinking O'Toole brought her to his trailer and gave her a shot of brandy to warm her up. He said she turned "roses and cream, bounced out of the caravan, radiated towards the motor car, hopped into it and drove off, taking with her five great big lamps, the trimmers of which had flung themselves on the cobbles out of the way."

The *New York Times'* Bosley Crowther called the film's plot and the "gaily eccentric" Givenchy wardrobe "clearly preposterous". But it set a non-holiday opening week record when shown at New York's Radio City Music Hall in July 1966. The film reviewer Judith Crist called it "an absolute strawberry-shortcake of a film, with Audrey Hepburn and Peter O'Toole an utterly delightful pair."

How to Steal a Million may have been as delicious as French patisserie, but Audrey's next film, *Two for the Road* (1967), would be a departure from the romantic flavour to something more experimental. A brittle study of marriage, it featured cruder language, semi-nude scenes and sex out of wedlock, and would be the first time she had appeared in her swimsuit on screen – "It is inconceivable that it could have been submitted to me ten years ago," she said. [81] Now that she was in her mid-thirties, she had evolved from the gamine roles. Mel convinced her that the romantic comedies, a staple of her career over the last 15 years, were becoming worn and there was a desire to create movies more akin to the French New Wave, or *Nouvelle Vague*, led by filmmakers François Truffaut, Jean-Luc Godard and Jacques Demy. With the collapse of Hollywood's studio system by the mid-sixties, and the relaxation of its constrictive censorship codes, young American filmmakers were looking to these European auteurs who created grittier, experimental works with a non-linear narrative, fragmented editing and a strong visual style.

Two for the Road was written by Frederic Raphael, screenwriter for *Darling* (1965), where its star, Julie Christie (playing a beautiful but amoral model Diana Scott), helped to establish the London Mod look. Owing a debt to the works of Truffaut and Godard, with its disjointed

Audrey with co-star Peter O'Toole, sitting on a
bench at the Rond-Point des Champs-Élysées.

Audrey enjoyed the company of
Peter O'Toole during the filming of
How to Steal a Million.

structure across five different times, Raphael's script was inspired by his and his wife's holidays to the South of France over many years. Travelling the same route, he often felt he was passing a former version of himself along the same road.

Raphael took the idea to the director Stanley Donen and then they both visited Audrey in Switzerland. She was enthusiastic about the concept, but having been burned by *Paris When It Sizzles* and its cuts in and out of a fantasy world, she was initially sceptical it would work. Still, she agreed to sign on. Raphael recalled, "Audrey wasn't prim, but she was what the French call 'pudique'. 'Modest', I suppose, is the nearest word." [82]

Audrey had told Donen she wanted Givenchy to dress her, but he explained that the young couple, Joanne and Mark, were comfortable, but not rich, and wouldn't be able to afford a top Parisian couture wardrobe. He thought that her clothes should be bought off the rack from hip boutiques and even when she took him to a Givenchy show to convince him otherwise, he was adamant. Audrey, with encouragement from Mel, reluctantly agreed. Designer Ken Scott was hired as fashion consultant, as well as providing some of his own designs, but Audrey's fastidiousness drove him to quit. He was replaced by British *Vogue* editor Lady Clare Rendlesham, who searched boutiques in Paris and London to find the perfect pret-à-porter. Items selected included Paco Rabanne's metallic shift dress, a yellow plastic visor cap, a PVC trouser suit and geometric pieces by Mary Quant. The film revealed a funkier Hepburn, away from the protective wrappings of Givenchy, and she was hailed as defying her age, even though she was still just in her mid-thirties.

Ladies' Home Journal in January 1967 featured Audrey Hepburn on the cover in one of her *Two for the Road* costumes, posing the question, "Is this really Audrey Hepburn? Would you believe she's 37?"

Once again, she was given an updated haircut, with a short and angular "do" which contrasted with the longer hair of the younger versions of the character. Alberto de Rossi also changed the shape of her eyebrows, claiming, "I've given her completely new eyes for this film."

Audrey's on-screen partner British actor Albert Finney (playing Mark Wallace) was 30 years old, seven years younger than her, and she loved his humour and his relaxed and impulsive behaviour, on and off set. Their free time together was spent feasting in little French bistros and his company was a welcome break from the troubles in her marriage. The making of the film was something of an awakening for her and just as her character has an affair with a Frenchman, it's thought her relationship with Finney crossed over into reality. There was a much-advertised nude bedroom scene, which was filmed at the Hôtel du Golf at Beauvallon, near St Tropez. She had been nervous to do it, but, in reality, it was very tame and she was covered by sheets.

"The Audrey I saw during the making of this film I didn't even know," said Stanley Donen. "She overwhelmed me. She was so free, so happy. I never saw her like that. So young! I don't think I was responsible. I guess it was Albie [Finney]." [83]

Reflecting the new permissiveness of the era she was living through, her next movie, *Wait Until Dark*, was similarly experimental. Released in October 1967, Audrey plays Susy Hendrix, a recently blinded woman terrorized by a gang of drug dealers, who believe there is a packet of heroin hidden in her apartment.

She wanted to shift her image to suit the changes in society; the loss of innocence and a cynicism as a result of the ongoing Vietnam War, societal discontent and civil rights movement protests. In Paris, there was continued unrest, which culminated in the May 1968 student rebellions. The Latin Quarter became a battleground between riot police and students, who were questioning capitalism and consumerism, and taking after the nineteenth-century Paris tradition of militancy, combined with sixties countercultural values.

Audrey as the younger Joanna in *Two for the Road* (1967) on the Plage du Brouis in the French Riviera.

Mel had encouraged Audrey to reinvent herself with *Two for the Road* and *Wait Until Dark*, but this new sense of freedom contributed towards the end of their marriage after 13 years, when she asked for a divorce. There had been many stories of his controlling nature, that he had scolded her like a child when she accidentally swore, and that he told her what roles she should accept or turn down, despite the frequent defence in the press that she was a woman of her own mind. He had also been jealous of her astronomical fame – "of course it's a problem, when the wife outshines the husband as Audrey does me," he once said. [84] The divorce came through in November 1968 and soon after, her life would change significantly. To recuperate after the stress of divorce, Audrey went on a long Mediterranean cruise with friends and it was here, on a private yacht, that she met a young Roman doctor, Andrea Dotti. On January 18, 1969, six weeks after her divorce from Mel was finalized, they were married in a private ceremony in the town hall of Morges, Switzerland. Audrey wore a short pink jersey mini-dress designed by Givenchy, with her hair covered by a matching headscarf. It was a fresh, modern ensemble that heralded a new era for the actress.

After their wedding, the Dottis moved to Rome, where they lived in a converted hill-top palazzo with views over the Tiber. Audrey chose to step away from the screen in favour of being a housewife and in 1970, she gave birth to their son, Luca. She settled into her life in Rome with Andrea, Sean and Luca, where she was Signora Dotti, an Italian wife and mother of two boys, who was captured by paparazzi in the city going shopping and collecting her children from school. Andrea was several years younger and still held a desire to be out on the town. At first, she tried to keep up with her husband by accompanying him to nightclubs, sitting at tables covered in bottles of fizz, and doing the twist, but she wasn't a night owl and, instead, he was frequently snapped by paparazzi with a series of beautiful young women while Audrey stayed at home. Perhaps he had expected her to be the girl from *Roman Holiday* and

Audrey wearing Paco Rabanne's
metallic silver disc dress, in a scene
from *Two for the Road*.

was disappointed to find the reality: a woman who preferred peace and tranquility to a hectic social life.

She missed Givenchy's collections in Paris, but as the mother of a young child, it wasn't possible to go to Paris on a whim. Instead, she bought a new wardrobe of modish clothes from Rome's hip boutiques on Via Frattina and Via Condotti, and while she suited the Mary Quant mini-dresses which complimented her angular hair, she still preferred Givenchy's clothing over everyone else.

Sergio Russo, a former assistant to Alexandre, the famous Parisian stylist, became Audrey's Italian hairdresser and by the early seventies, with the popularity of the hippie deluxe style of the European jet set, she adapted her wardrobe to suit her location, mixing Givenchy coats and Valentino dresses. Rome in the late sixties and early seventies was considered a dangerous place. It was no longer the Rome of

"THE CITIES ARE NOT A PLACE FOR YOU IF YOU ARE FAMOUS"

Fellini's *La Dolce Vita*, as the Red Brigade attacked buildings and the city's wealthiest residents faced kidnapping threats. For safety reasons, Audrey decided to send her sons to school in Switzerland and she moved back to her beloved farmhouse, which she had kept following her divorce from Mel, and visited her husband in Rome at the weekends. According to her son, Sean, she was aware of Andrea's philandering and it was incredibly painful to her. Still, she worked to keep her marriage intact and continued to choose family over career. [85]

"The cities are not a place for you if you are famous," she said. "With the paparazzi in Rome, there is no privacy.... It is because I live in the country in Switzerland that I can lead a totally unself-conscious life and be totally myself."

The costumes in *Two for the Road* were Audrey's most cutting-edge. Here she browses clothing with Mel Ferrer on the French Riviera.

CHAPTER NINE

Paris is a Moveable Feast

AUDREY MAY HAVE PRACTICED RESTRAINT
WHEN IT CAME TO FOOD, AS SHE WAS
CONSCIOUS OF MAINTAINING HER
NATURALLY SLIM FRAME TO AN IDEAL
WEIGHT, BUT HER TASTES WERE DECIDEDLY
PARISIAN – STEAKS, CHEESE SOUFFLÉ AND
RASPBERRY COMPÔTE.

According to her close friend and neighbour in Switzerland, Doris Brynner (wife of the actor Yul Brynner), the actress adored spaghetti and vanilla ice cream served with fudge sauce and they'd spend many delightful afternoons chatting over lunch together. Despite occasional indulgences, such as a glass of whisky in the evening, her preferences were for simple, good food and the press frequently listed her diet, as if it would be aspirational to readers who wanted to maintain their figures.

"She always eats the same breakfast," reported *Good Housekeeping* in 1959. "Two boiled eggs, one piece of seven-grain whole-wheat toast from a health-food store, and three or four cups of coffee laced with hot milk. Her lunch consists of cottage cheese and fruit salad or of yoghurt with raw vegetables. For dinner, she has meat and several cooked vegetables."

A similar article in *Cosmopolitan* in 1959 reported on her devotion to a form of yoga, which was described as "feeling like an animal". She

"WHEN AUDREY FOUND SOMEWHERE SHE LOVED, SHE LIKED TO VISIT IT AGAIN AND AGAIN."

was photographed by Bob Willoughby, dressed in a red leotard as she practiced "animal" inspired stretches, which were adapted yoga poses.

Audrey was a homebody and so when she was in Paris, her life tended to follow a reassuring pattern, where she would be early to bed with a good book and early to rise, as she often had to report to the studio first thing. "It's fun to unlock my door and find the new record that the store down the street has delivered during the afternoon," she once said of her time in Los Angeles. "I get into old, soft, comfy clothes and then I play the new music while I cook. I'm into steaks. Boy, those Californian sirloin steaks!" [86]

This preferred way of living transferred to wherever she was in the world, including in Paris. As demonstrated by her 40-year loyalty to Givenchy, when Audrey found somewhere she loved, she liked to visit it again and again. These are some of the places she spent time in when in Paris.

Audrey in the Restaurant Lasserre, Paris, with
Hubert de Givenchy, after the premiere of *My
Fair Lady* in December 1964.

PREVIOUS Audrey in a Parisian restaurant
in 1955.

The Art Nouveau restaurant Maxim's de Paris
was one of Audrey's favourite places to dine.

The Hotel Raphaël

Of all the places to stay in Paris, it was the Hotel Raphaël that was Audrey's retreat. She enjoyed relaxing in the ground-floor mahogany-panelled bar with its plush velvet seats and fusion lighting, and where the bartender knew how she liked her martini to be fixed. The Art Deco hotel, located on Avenue Kléber, close to the Champs-Élysées, was built in 1925, at the height of the Roaring Twenties, or the *Années folles* as it was known in France, and was named in tribute to the Renaissance painter. It attracted a prestigious Hollywood guest list, including Ava Gardner, Clark Gable, Henry Fonda, Grace Kelly and Gary Cooper.

During filming of *Paris When It Sizzles*, she and William Holden relaxed on the top-floor private terrace, which was dotted with plants and clinging vines, and offered amazing views of the Arc de Triomphe and the Eiffel Tower.

The Ritz Paris, Place Vendôme

The most famous luxury hotel in Paris, and the permanent home of Coco Chanel for almost 40 years, the Ritz Paris is located at 15 Place Vendôme in the heart of the fashion district. It was first opened in 1898 by Swiss hotelier César Ritz, who created a space that offered the utmost discretion and comfort for his guests, with apricot-soft lighting and marble, wood and gold interiors. By the twenties it stood for all things modern and extravagant. The writer F. Scott Fitzgerald dreamed of diamonds "as big as the Ritz", Irving Berlin wrote the song, "Puttin' on the Ritz" and the novelist Ernest Hemingway once said: "When in Paris, the only reason not to stay at The Ritz is if you can't afford it."

It featured a discreetly dark mahogany bar, which was the favourite spot for Hemingway after Paris's liberation in 1944, an outdoor courtyard, Ritz Bar, accessed by its rue Cambon entrance and featured in *How to Steal a Million*, and a fine dining room, which attracted Paris's elite.

Maxim's de Paris, 3 rue Royale

Maxim's restaurant, located on the fashionable rue Royale, first opened in 1893 and the little bistro quickly became the "in" place to dine in Belle Époque Paris, attracting an eclectic crowd of courtesans, actors, politicians and artists. In 1900 it was further transformed into an Art Nouveau masterpiece with romantic murals and swirling gold embellishments, gilded mirrors and red velvet seats. In the 1920s the Lost Generation (*see also* page 23) would visit for a nostalgic trip back to the 1900s and by the fifties and sixties, it was the restaurant of choice for the Duke and Duchess of Windsor, Greta Garbo, Jacqueline Kennedy and Brigitte Bardot, who arrived in a Rolls-Royce and entered scandalously barefoot, with her father, Louis Bardot, and then-husband, Gunther Sachs, in tow.

L'Orangerie Paris, Île Saint-Louis

Audrey visited this traditional French restaurant with her friends, the model Capucine and designer Hubert de Givenchy, in the late sixties and early seventies. The restaurant was located on a narrow street on the Île Saint Louis and offered an intimate and cosy dining experience.

Restaurant Lasserre, 17 Avenue Franklin Roosevelt

Only a hop from the Champs-Élysées, Lasserre was founded by chef René Lasserre in 1942 and was awarded two Michelin stars by 1951. With French delicacies, including *canard à l'orange*, flambéed veal kidneys and truffle foie gras, it was a favourite of the rich and influential in Paris. As well as Audrey and her first husband, Mel Ferrer, frequent guests at the restaurant included such luminaries as Salvador Dalí, Marc Chagall and Jean Renoir. It was the location for a celebratory dinner to mark the Paris premiere of *My Fair Lady* in December 1964, where Audrey was pictured seated next to Hubert de Givenchy.

Lucas Carton, 9 Place de la Madeleine

One of the most exclusive restaurants in Paris, the Lucas Carton is situated on the Place de la Madeleine. Dating back to 1839, the restaurant was considered the fashionable spot in Napoleon III's Paris, when it was known as La Taverne de France. In the 1880s the interior was transformed with Art Nouveau carved wood sculptures and mirrors, and in the years following the First World War it became a popular place for politicians to dine.

One evening during the filming of *Love in the Afternoon*, Audrey and her then-husband Mel were dining with the French actor Charles Boyer. When a dessert of *Crêpes Suzette* was brought to their table by the maître d' ready to be set alight with Grand Marnier, Audrey asked that she be allowed to flambé the pancakes herself.

Angelina Paris, 226 rue de Rivoli

It's believed that Audrey would occasionally stop into Angelina when in the fashion district of Paris – a tea room and pâtisserie famous for its rich and creamy hot chocolate and delectable Mont Blanc, a chestnut, cream and meringue gateau. The Art Nouveau tea room, with its tranquil wall art, dates back to 1903, when it was opened by a confectioner, Antoine Rumpelmayer, who hired a Belle Époque architect, Édouard-Jean Niermans, to create an elegant and romantic interior.

OVERLEAF Audrey with Mel Ferrer in 1955,
getting into a car on the Place Vendôme,
outside The Ritz Paris.

CHAPTER TEN

Creating the Legend

"PEOPLE ASSOCIATE ME WITH A TIME WHEN
WOMEN WORE PRETTY DRESSES IN FILMS
AND YOU HEARD BEAUTIFUL MUSIC," AUDREY
SAID. "NOW PEOPLE ARE FRIGHTENED BY THE
MOVIES. *ROBIN AND MARIAN* IS REALLY ABOUT
HOW MUCH TWO PEOPLE LOVE EACH OTHER.
IT'S AN INTIMATE STORY AND THAT'S WHY I
WANTED TO DO IT." [87]

"Everything I had been offered before then was too kinky, too violent or too young," she said. "I had been playing ingénues since the early fifties and I thought it would be wonderful to play somebody of my own age in something romantic and lovely." [88]

By the seventies, there were scant opportunities for good female roles in movies as scripts tended to focus on men and their relationships with one another. Audrey had opted to step aside from film-making for the best part of a decade, but in that time, many of the top stars who had ruled the box office in the fifties and early sixties fought to stay relevant. It was a struggle for actresses, and particularly older actresses, to find quality parts, and they were typically resigned to disaster films or low-budget horrors.

When Audrey received the script for *Robin and Marian* in 1975, it stood out among the many others she was frequently sent. She was to play an older Maid Marian who rekindles a romance with Sean Connery's Robin Hood and it would be directed by Richard Lester on location in Spain.

Despite her wish for a happy home and her commitment to caring for her children in Switzerland and visiting her husband in Rome, Andrea Dotti was frequently unfaithful to his wife, with the paparazzi photos splashed in newspapers as proof. [89] It was with a desire to gain back some control that she decided to make her long-awaited return to film. Audrey was also once again visible at awards ceremonies and events around the world, where she felt confident in her luxury armour of Givenchy couture. She made frequent returns to Paris, where she would be fitted for her gowns at the Avenue George V salon.

In 1975 she appeared at the 47th Academy Awards in Los Angeles wearing a white Givenchy gown with a beaded bodice, which offered a daring glimpse of her midriff. Then in March 1976, she arrived in Hollywood with Andrea Dotti to present her *Roman Holiday* and *How to Steal a Million* director William Wyler with his Life Achievement Award from the American Film Institute and wowed in red Givenchy. She and Dotti stopped in New York on the way back to Europe for the

Captured by paparazzi on the streets of Paris
with her son, Sean Ferrer.

PREVIOUS Audrey photographed in 1957,
perfectly at home in Paris.

premiere of *Robin and Marian* at Radio City Music Hall. Thousands of supporters came out to see her, presenting her with orchids and white roses. "We love you, dear Audrey," they chanted. With each appearance, she radiated a magical aura. She was still incredibly chic, but she possessed a warmth in how she interacted with people and it was this down-to-earth quality, combined with timeless Parisian elegance, that made her so adored.

At this point she considered acting to be more like a hobby as being there for her children was much more of a priority: "The older you get, the more you have to resign yourself to not working or taking inconsequential or frightening parts," she said. One film she said yes to was *Bloodline* (1979), based on the best-selling novel by Sidney Sheldon, although she may have regretted it on seeing the finished product. With nudity and gory scenes, it was the only R-rated film of her career.

"PARIS!" SHE EXCLAIMS OVER THE PHONE. "I'D LOVE IT."

Her character, Elizabeth Roffe, is a pharmaceutical heiress who is the target of a killer, who has already murdered her father. While the Elizabeth of the novel was just 23, with Audrey being almost 50, her character's age was changed to 35. To illustrate Elizabeth's role as a global businesswoman, it was filmed in a number of locations around the world, including New York, Zurich, Sardinia and Paris.

Elizabeth receives a late-night phone call from her new husband, Rhys Williams (Ben Gazzara), having agreed to a marriage of convenience. He invites her to go with him to Paris and she hopes to take their relationship further: "Paris!" she exclaims over the phone. "I'd love it."

Some scenes in the mystery/thriller *Bloodline* (1979) were filmed in Paris, with Notre-Dame as a backdrop, and in the restaurant Maxim's.

On arrival in the city they check into the George V Hotel. It's cold, so she wears smart trousers, a tweed jacket and carries a beige overcoat. They walk along the Pont de la Tournelle, with a view of Notre-Dame in the background, and dine together at Maxim's, the exclusive Art Nouveau restaurant that Audrey would frequent in real life. Romy Schneider's character – Hélène Roffe-Martin, the villain in a black leather Gucci coat – stays in a stunning art-filled apartment with a view to the Arc de Triomphe from the living room window.

Elizabeth is rich, attractive and sophisticated and so Hubert de Givenchy was tasked with creating the 14 outfits required for the character, from simple tailored suits and silk blouses for the boardroom to a powder-blue satin wedding gown, a shimmering black lace cocktail dress and diaphanous nightgowns. The most stunning outfit, a daring sheer black evening gown with flowered beading over the left breast, was designed for the love scene in Maxim's. While dining, she is confronted by her husband's glamorous former girlfriends and the dress illustrates that she can hold her own against any woman. He follows her outside the restaurant and they embrace under the grand columns of rue Royale, with the illuminated fountain of Place de la Concorde in the background. As critic and columnist Rex Reed said, "At fifty, Audrey Hepburn is still vulnerable and doe-like, the perfect victim in Givenchy clothes."

On the first day of shooting, Audrey observed how reverential everyone was towards her, as if she was a member of royalty among the international cast. "Why is everyone so worshipful?" she wondered aloud.[90] As well as starring James Mason, the male lead in the film was Ben Gazzara, an Italian-American character actor, and her female co-stars Romy Schneider, Michelle Phillips and Irene Papas were well-known figures in European cinema, but it was Audrey who was the star.

During a publicity event for *Bloodline*, held at Maxim's, she told a reporter: "Mostly I buy things in boutiques, and jeans are my way of life. If I'm in the garden, I would wear my oldest jeans, obviously, and to go shopping, I would probably wear pressed ones. I just don't dress up

Audrey leaving the L'Orangerie Restaurant on
L'île St Louis, Paris, with Hubert de Givenchy
and the actress-model Capucine.

anymore. And I don't buy couture, because it's become terribly, terribly expensive. Dressing with a capital 'D' is for important occasions. For that, I always come to Hubert [Givenchy]." [91]

The film, and Terence Young's direction, was panned by critics, particularly as it was a far cry from the innocence and glamour of her Paris-set movies. Roger Ebert wrote in the *Chicago Sun-Times*: "After six months, a week, and two days of suspense, we can now relax: The worst movie of 1979 has opened ... See Sidney Sheldon's *Bloodline*, and weep for the cinema."

There was little to celebrate about the film, except for her wardrobe. Despite previous issues with Givenchy's relationship with Audrey, Paramount's legendary costume designer Edith Head was willing to offer them praise: "Audrey and Givenchy have a special rapport. Explain the charisma? It's difficult, although it's perfectly apparent when you watch her on the screen. She has a certain charm, a certain fashion instinct that no matter what she puts on, she makes it look divine. She is a professional actress who realizes that in dressing for a part she isn't dressing to please herself, but to transform herself into a character." [92]

Audrey kept the $200,000 worth of Givenchy clothing from the film and she took some of these garments with her on a second honeymoon to Hawaii with Andrea, in the hope it could put the spark back into their marriage. As much as his infidelity was painful, she had initially wished to hold the marriage together until her younger son Luca was old enough to cope with the divorce. [93] "I tried desperately to avoid it," she said. "I hung on in both marriages very hard, as long as I could, for the children's sake, and out of respect for marriage." [94] When it became clear the relationship was irreparable, she agreed to star in Peter Bogdanovich's romantic comedy *They All Laughed* (1981) as a cure for a broken heart. He pitched it to her as a film in the mode of her romantic movies of the fifties, like *Sabrina* and *Love in the Afternoon*, and it seemed particularly appealing after the disaster of *Bloodline*.

She played a woman who feels neglected in her marriage to a

tycoon and so goes to New York as a means of change. Her husband hires a private detective (reuniting her with Ben Gazzara) to watch over her and during the course of the film, they fall in love. Shooting began in New York, in April 1979, and the look Bogdanovich envisioned for her was a wardrobe of non-Givenchy street clothes, with simple trench coats, headscarves, jeans and pea-jackets. As he recalled, he encouraged her to wear the clothes she was most familiar with. "She took me upstairs to her suite at the [hotel] Pierre, opened the closet and slid all her clothes out on to the bed. And there and then we selected the ones she would wear in the film," Bogdanovich said. [95]

After her second divorce was finalized in 1982, Audrey came into her own once more. She had met and fallen in love with a Dutchman, Robert (Robbie) Wolders, a television actor who was the widower of the late actress Merle Oberon, and he helped make Audrey feel more confident and content than ever: "It was clear that Robbie and I had found each other at a time in our lives when we were both very unhappy. And now we're terribly happy again," she said in 1991. [96]

Audrey made frequent appearances at memorial dinners, galas and award ceremonies, where she was celebrated as a living treasure. The 1980s was a time when people looked with nostalgia at the Golden Age of Hollywood and the studio star system that created the mystery and glamour of icons like Audrey was revered. "I never considered myself as having much talent, or looks, or anything else. I fell into this career. I was unknown, insecure, inexperienced, and skinny. I worked very hard – that I'll take credit for – but I don't understand any of it. At the same time, it warms me. I'm terribly touched by it," she told *Vanity Fair.* [97]

She still had the muscle tone from her ballet training and she wore her hair simply, to accentuate those razor-sharp cheekbones. During this time she found herself having to contend with increasingly brazen interviewers and talk show hosts questioning her about her body, as if she had to justify her figure. But always, she answered with grace.

In May 1982, New York's Fashion Institute of Technology held a retrospective exhibition celebrating 30 years of Hubert de Givenchy. Audrey flew in as guest of honour, wearing a black satin one-shoulder gown he had designed for the occasion. As part of this event, and the touring exhibition that followed, Audrey's Paris films, and the costumes Givenchy created for her on screen, were celebrated once more.

"We would create together," Givenchy reflected in 1989. "With the influence of Audrey and my sketches we did the 'Sabrina' décolleté, all the T-shirts, all the black dresses from *Breakfast at Tiffany's*. Now, what is so funny is that the line of that period is popular with young people again ... they want to remember that now." [98]

The last time Audrey was dressed by Givenchy on-screen was in 1987, for a television romance/thriller called *Love Among Thieves* (1987) in which she co-starred with Robert Wagner. The movie shared similarities with *Charade* and *How to Steal a Million* and in it she played an aristocratic concert pianist, Baroness Caroline DuLac, who is forced to steal a priceless Fabergé egg collection as ransom for her kidnapped fiancé. Wagner plays Mike Chambers, the art dealer on her trail, who follows her from Paris to Mexico. She said she accepted the role "for the fun of it". [99]

In October 1985, Audrey Hepburn attended the "Oscars de la Mode" at the opera house in Paris, in the company of Givenchy, as they walked up the same steps she strode down in *Funny Face*. The event, organized by the French federation of couture, presented Audrey with an award for her loyalty to the designer and she wore a Spanish-inspired dress with bright swirls on a black background. She enjoyed these glamorous events in Paris, and in December 1986 was accompanied by Robbie Wolders, French banker Guy de Rothschild and his wife Marie-Hélène for a gala event at the Moulin Rouge, where she shimmered in black Givenchy. She was also a frequent

Audrey with Givenchy at an event at the Paris Opera in October 1985.

presence at Givenchy's twice-yearly Paris collections, cheering him on, while he, in turn, would pay tribute to Hepburn, with many of his designs created with her in mind.

In 1987 Audrey arrived in Paris to receive the Commander of the Order of Arts and Letters from the Minister of Culture and the event, and the promise of seeing Audrey, brought excited crowds to cheer her and fellow luminary Sean Connery, who was awarded at the same time. That same year, the Museum of Modern Art in New York held a gala in Audrey's honour, with the aim of raising money for the Film Preservation Fund. The dinner was the first major tribute to her career and she wore a black silk Givenchy dress with a jacket embroidered with tiny white beads. "This evening is really for our children, because only the magic of movies can show them one day how we were – our history, our spirit, maybe even our dreams," she told guests. It was a prescient observation as the focus for the remainder of her life was to raise awareness for the suffering of children around the world, a cause she held dear.

In March 1988 Audrey was in Tokyo to attend a gala in aid of UNICEF and she was approached by the charity to be their special ambassador, following the death of their previous ambassador, actor Danny Kaye. It would become an all-consuming role for her, but she was desperate to do all she could to help malnourished children, having had her own first-hand experience during the Second World War. Two weeks after her appointment, she embarked on her first assignment for the charity, travelling to the famine-inflicted Ethiopia with her partner Robbie Wolders. She chose a simple travelling uniform of chino pants, a headscarf, a Lacoste shirt, and if it was chilly at night, a pale turtleneck sweater. She wasn't involved to receive attention for herself, rather she wanted the focus to be on helping children.

Audrey was always the perfect muse for Givenchy, pictured here on the balcony of his spectacular home, the Hôtel d'Orrouer, Paris.

Despite her devotion to UNICEF, which took her on exhaustive trips to war-torn and famine-afflicted regions around the world, she continued to be a special guest at film premieres, charity galas and at the Academy Awards, where she was a vision in glittering Givenchy designs, which often reflected the glitzier aesthetic for the eighties. In 1990 she was presented with the Cecil B. DeMille Award at the 1990 Golden Globes, wearing cream satin Givenchy to collect her award from *Roman Holiday* co-star Gregory Peck, where she said, "I've been given a career that brought me nothing but fun and friends and happiness."

In April 1991, the San Francisco department store I. Magnin & Company held a charity ball in honour of Hubert de Givenchy. At the end of the fashion show, as the designer took a bow, the strains of "Moon River" began playing and Audrey came down the runway in

"I'VE BEEN GIVEN A CAREER THAT BROUGHT ME NOTHING BUT FUN AND FRIENDS AND HAPPINESS."

AUDREY HEPBURN

a simple white gown. They both received a standing ovation. Their close bond was demonstrated when on her sixtieth birthday, in 1989, Givenchy delivered 60 pure white rosebushes to La Paisable, where she planted them in the garden. He did the same in the garden of Le Jonchet, his seventeenth-century mansion near Tours, as a way of being close to one another, even when apart.

In 1988 Givenchy sold his label to the luxury fashion conglomerate LVMH Moët Hennessy Louis Vuitton and just after the deal was signed, he arrived in California to be presented with the state's first Lifetime Achievement award for his 36 years in the business. Audrey was there by his side as she spoke about their loyal friendship and collaborations over the years. While he continued on as lead designer, the deal gave him more time to pursue his passion for interior design. In 1986 he had purchased from a friend the second floor of the spectacular Hôtel d'Orrouer, a Parisian Regency building dating

To celebrate the 40th anniversary of
Givenchy's label, Audrey wore a design from
his Autumn/Winter 1991–92 collection.

from 1732 and located on the rue de Grenelle. A few years later he snapped up the rest of the building and lovingly transformed it into a haven with his beloved antique furniture, chic patterned wallpaper and valuable paintings. Audrey continued to be his muse and for the Autumn/Winter 1991/92 collection, she modelled his gowns, posing on the balcony of his home overlooking the lush gardens and on the elegant sofa in his emerald living room.

In late 1992, after having suffered excruciating stomach pains, Audrey was diagnosed with incurable cancer. She had been travelling extensively with UNICEF and by the time she underwent tests in a clinic in Los Angeles, the prognosis was that there was nothing that could be done. Audrey wanted to spend her final days in Switzerland, surrounded by family, but she was told travel would be too risky for her. Givenchy stepped in to help by giving her a final gift, the loan of a private jet to carefully take her home. It was at her beloved La Paisable that she passed away on January 20, 1993, with her two sons and partner Robbie Wolders by her side. She was just 63 years old.

In her many obituaries, Audrey was frequently described as "aristocratic", "gamine" and, in the *New York Times*, as "the lithe young thing with stars in her eyes and the ability to make Cinderella transformations". Over the years, she was given almost mythical status as an angelic human, a woman in possession of incomparable style and with innate grace and charm.

Her beatnik look from *Funny Face*, with the black turtleneck sweater, flat shoes and slim trousers, continued to be hailed as the "intellectual fashion" for the 1950s and would later be revived in a Gap commercial. Audrey's Parisian essence continues to live on, in the chicest little black dress, in the garret of a Left Bank apartment, and with the simple pleasures of strolling along the Seine, or looking out across the city from the highest point in Montmartre.

Audrey's unique spirit and energy lives on in
Paris, as personified by her bohemian dance
in a club in *Funny Face*.

Index

219

Endnotes

1 Drake, Nicholas, *The Fifties in Vogue* (Henry Holt & Co, 1987)

2 Lehman West, Beverley, *Finding My Way Back to 1950s Paris* (Cellar Door Press, 2014)

3 Montgomery, Ann, *Another Me: A Memoir* (iUniverse, 2008)

4 *Vanity Fair*, Hepburn Heart, Dominick Dunne, May 1991

5 Zolotow, Maurice, *Billy Wilder in Hollywood*, (Putnam, 1977)

6 Woodward, Ian, *Audrey Hepburn: Fair Lady of the Screen* (Chivers, Windsor, Paragon & Co, 1994)

7 Quoted in Woodward, Ian, *Audrey Hepburn: Fair Lady of the Screen* (Chivers, Windsor, Paragon & Co, 1994)

8 Paris, Barry, *Audrey Hepburn* (Weidenfeld & Nicholson, 1997)

9 Picardie, Justine, *Miss Dior: A Wartime Story of Courage and Couture* (Faber & Faber, 2021)

10 Walker, Alexander, *Audrey: Her Real Story* (St Martins Press, 1995)

11 Academy of Motion Pictures Arts and Sciences, Paramount Pictures production records

12 *Vogue* magazine, Audrey Hepburn by Cecil Beaton, November 1954

13 Paris, Barry, *Audrey Hepburn* (Weidenfeld & Nicholson, 1997)

14 The *New York Times*, Why Has She Done so Few Films in Recent Years? Michiko Kakutani, June 4, 1980

15 Wasson, Sam, *Fifth Avenue, 5AM: Audrey Hepburn, Breakfast at Tiffany's, and the Dawn of the Modern Woman* (Harper Perennial, 2021)

16 Hellstern, Melissa, *How to be Lovely: The Audrey Hepburn Way of Life* (Portico, 2002)

17 Calistro, Paddy, *Edith Head's Hollywood* (Angel City Press, 2009)

18 Academy of Motion Pictures Arts and Sciences, Margaret Herrick Library, Paramount Pictures production files

19 The *Journal News*, Pigtails New Departure for Audrey Hepburn in *Styles*, October 18, 1956

20 *Vanity Fair*, When Hubert met Audrey, Amy Fine Collins, February 3, 2014

21 The *New York Times*, Hubert de Givenchy on Audrey Hepburn, Dana Thomas, March 13, 2018

22 *Vanity Fair*, When Hubert met Audrey, Amy Fine Collins, February 3, 2014

23 The *New York Times*, Hubert de Givenchy on Audrey Hepburn, Dana Thomas, March 13, 2018

24 Academy of Motion Pictures Arts and Sciences, Margaret Herrick Library, Paramount Pictures production files

25 *Vanity Fair*, When Hubert met Audrey, Amy Fine Collins, February 3, 2014

26 *Independent*, Passions of an Ingenue Who Never Grows Old, Angela Lambert, 26 January 1993

27 The *New York Times*, Half Nympth, Half Wunderkind, Helen Markel Herrmann, February 14, 1954

28 *The New York Times*, Sabrina review, Bosley Crowther, September 23, 1954

29 *Silver Screen*, Is Hollywood Shifting its accent on sex? Earl Wilson, July 1954

30 *Photoplay*, The Small, Private World of Audrey Hepburn, Mary W Jones, February 1957

31 Paris, Barry, *Audrey Hepburn* (Weidenfeld & Nicholson, 1997)

32 *New York Post*, Audrey's Advice: Have Fun, Let Hubby Wear the Pants, Sidney Skolsky, August 19, 1957

33 Silverman, Stephen, *Dancing on the Ceiling* (Alfred A Knopf, 1995)

34 BBC archive, unedited interview with Stanley Donen, 1974

35 *Vanity Fair*, Anything Goes for Oscar, Amy Fine Collins, March 1998

36 Paris, Barry, *Audrey Hepburn* (Weidenfeld & Nicholson, 1997)

37 *Dance Magazine*, William Hawkins, October 1956

38 Paris, Barry, *Audrey Hepburn* (Weidenfeld & Nicholson, 1997)

39 *Photoplay*, The Small, Private World of Audrey Hepburn, Mary W Jones, February 1957

40 Academy of Motion Pictures Arts and Sciences, Margaret Herrick Library, Paramount Pictures production files

41 The *New York Times*, On the Seine in the Rain with 'Funny Face', W Granger Blair, July 15, 1956

42 *Harper's Bazaar*, All About Audrey, Pamela Fiori, January 23, 2013

43 BBC archive, unedited interview with Stanley Donen, 1974

44 Lehman West, *Beverley, Finding My Way Back to 1950s Paris* (Cellar Door Press, 2014)

45 *World Telegram*, Audrey Keeps Park in a Stir, William Pepper, August 26, 1957

46 The *New York Times*, Hubert de Givenchy on Audrey Hepburn, Dana Thomas, 13 March 2018

47 The *Journal News*, Pigtails New Departure for Audrey Hepburn in *Styles*. October 18 1956

48 The *Cincinnati Enquirer*, Audrey Hepburn, Hubert Givenchy: Fashion's Dream Team, Jill Gerston, July 9, 1979

49 The *Journal News*, Pigtails New Departure for Audrey Hepburn in *Styles*. October 18 1956

50 *American Cinematographer*, High Key vs Low Key, Frederick Foster, August 1957

51 *Apollo Magazine*, The Many Faces of Audrey Hepburn, Rosalind McKever, July 9, 2015

52 *Evening Standard*, I Look at Love, Sept 22, 1956

53 The *Baltimore Sun*, Ageless Beauty, Timeless Fashion, Genevieve Buck, September 21, 1989

54 The *Spokesman-Review*, Paris Styles, Please, Audrey, Lydia Lane, May 10, 1959

55 Paris, Barry, *Audrey Hepburn* (Weidenfeld & Nicholson, 1997)

56 Woodward, Ian, A*udrey Hepburn: Fair Lady of the Screen* (Chivers, Windsor, Paragon & co, 1994)
57 Walker, Alexander, *Audrey: Her Real Story* (St Martins Press, 1995)
58 *W Magazine*, The Unparalleled Elegance of Hubert de Givenchy, William Middleton, May 16, 2022
59 *Daily News*, Paris Film Romp for Holden, Hepburn, Dorothy Masters, 08 July 1962
60 The *Philadelphia Inquirer*, Givenchy, Hepburn co-star, Rubye Graham, 14 August 1962
61 *Press and Sun-Bulletin*, My Fair Lady Calls Audrey From the Paris She Loves, Henry Gris, 12 Jan 1963
62 The *Austin American*, People, Lloyd J Mathews Jr, 13 August 1962
63 Higham, Charles, *Audrey: The Life of Audrey Hepburn* (New York, 1984)
64 The *Philadelphia Inquirer*, Givenchy, Hepburn co-star, Rubye Graham, 14 August 1962
65 The *New York Times*, Americans Shoot 'Paris' When it Drizzles, Halsey Raines, 23 September 1962
66 *St Louis Globe-Democrat*, Audrey Plans Ahead, 09 November 1962
67 *St Louis Globe-Democrat*, Audrey Plans Ahead, 09 November 1962
68 Curtis, Tony and Paris, Barry, *Tony Curtis: The Autobiography* (William Morrow & Co, 1993)
69 *Press and Sun-Bulletin*, My Fair Lady Calls Audrey From the Paris She Loves, Henry Gris, 12 Jan 1963
70 Walker, Alexander, *Audrey: Her Real Story* (St Martins Press, 1995)
71 Silverman, Stephen, *Dancing on the Ceiling* (Alfred A Knopf, 1995)
72 *Press and Sun-Bulletin*, My Fair Lady Calls Audrey From the Paris She Loves, Henry Gris, 12 Jan 1963
73 *American Cinematographer*, The Photography of Charade, Herb A Lightman, May 1964
74 *American Cinematographer*, The Photography of Charade, Herb A Lightman, May 1964
75 *New York Herald Tribune Service*, Audrey Hepburn Near Perfection, Eugenia Sheppard, December 18, 1963
76 *New York Herald Tribune Service*, Audrey Hepburn Near Perfection, Eugenia Sheppard, December 18, 1963
77 The *New York Times*, Co-stars again: Audrey Hepburn and Givenchy, Gloria Emerson, 8 September 1965
78 The *New York Times*, Actress Has Influential Fashion Role, Bernadine Morris, December 14, 1963
79 The *Los Angeles Times*, Givenchy: Retrospective for Art Education, October 28, 1988
80 Paris, Barry, *Audrey Hepburn* (Weidenfeld & Nicholson, 1997)
81 Walker, Alexander, *Audrey: Her Real Story* (St Martins Press, 1995)
82 Woodward, Ian, *Audrey Hepburn: Fair Lady of the Screen* (Chivers, Windsor, Paragon & co, 1994)
83 Spoto, Donald, *Enchantment: The Life of Audrey Hepburn* (Arrow, 2007)
84 Conversation with Sean Ferrer by this author for *Roman Holiday: The Secret Life of Hollywood in Rome* (The History Press, 2018)
85 Paris, Barry, *Audrey Hepburn* (Weidenfeld & Nicholson, 1997)
86 *Photoplay*, Knee-deep in Stardust, Pauline Swanson, April 1954
87 Paris, Barry, *Audrey Hepburn* (Weidenfeld & Nicholson, 1997)
88 The *Philadelphia Inquirer*, On Movies, Desmond Ryan, July 30, 1979
89 Conversation with Sean Ferrer by this author for *Roman Holiday: The Secret Life of Hollywood in Rome* (The History Press, 2018)
90 The *Ottawa Journal*, M. George Haddad, June 28, 1979
91 The *Cincinnati Enquirer*, Audrey Hepburn, Hubert Givenchy: Fashion's Dream Team, Jill Gerston, 9 July 1979
92 The *Cincinnati Enquirer*, Audrey Hepburn, Hubert Givenchy: Fashion's Dream Team, Jill Gerston, 9 July 1979
93 Conversation with Sean Ferrer by this author for *Roman Holiday: The Secret Life of Hollywood in Rome* (The History Press, 2018)
94 *US* magazine, Glenn Plaskin, Audrey Hepburn, October 17, 1988
95 Paris, Barry, *Audrey Hepburn* (Weidenfeld & Nicholson, 1997)
96 *Vanity Fair*, Hepburn Heart, Dominick Dunne, May 1991
97 *Vanity Fair*, Hepburn Heart, Dominick Dunne, May 1991
98 The *Baltimore Sun*, Ageless Beauty, Timeless Fashion, Genevieve Buck, 21 September 1989
99 Woodward, Ian, *Audrey Hepburn: Fair Lady of the Screen* (Chivers, Windsor, Paragon & co, 1994)

Credits